VICHAI

The man who made dreams real

Andy Greeves

A Pillar Box Red Publication

© 2019. Published by Pillar Box Red Publishing Ltd.
Printed in the UK.

ISBN: 978-1-907823-62-6

Acknowledgements

The events of October 27, 2018 shocked and saddened so many people around the world, not least the players, staff and supporters at Leicester City Football Club and the wider Leicestershire community.

I offer my deepest and heartfelt condolences to the family and friends of Vichai Srivaddhanaprabha, as well as those connected to the other victims of the helicopter crash - Nusara Suknamai, Kaveporn Punpare, Eric Swaffer and Izabela Roza Lechowicz.

I would like to express a huge thanks to each and every person who took the time to speak to me during the process of writing this book.

To talkSPORT's Geoff Peters, who gave such touching words for the foreword to this title. To Ian Bason, Chairman of the Foxes Trust, who not only provided me with a fascinating interview but was a constant source of help as I sent various email questions back and forth! More information on the Foxes Trust can be found at foxestrust.co.uk.

Thank you to Oliver Winter, a close friend of Vichai's and President of the German Polo Association, who also agreed to be interviewed. A special thanks also to Debbie Alderstein, Nicholas Colquhoun-Denvers, Nick Rust and Nattabhumi Laosathirawong and huge apologies if I have forgotten to mention anyone else.

A final big thank you to my wife Cathryn and my son, Henry for their support and patience in me writing this book. Thoughts always to my late son Toby, who passed away in August 2014, aged just 23 days.

On November 6, 2018, the LCFC Foxes Foundation was renamed the Vichai Srivaddhanaprabha Foundation. You can donate to the Foundation, which has raised around £2m for Leicestershire charities at the time of writing, by visiting www.justgiving.com/VSfoundation.

Andy Greeves @AndyGreeves April 2019

In memory of Vichai Srivaddhanaprabha
April 4, 1958 – October 27, 2018

Contents

Foreword

Foreword

By Geoff Peters
talkSPORT Presenter and Match Reporter

"Vichai had a dream…"

The opening words to a football chant which has been sung with real gusto and emotion since the tragedy which saw the Leicester City owner and four others lose their lives.

Not many owners are shown the kind of love Vichai Srivaddhanaprabha received but he was adored on a massive scale and rightly so. Leicester City, a largely unfashionable club who for most of their existence bounced fairly unspectacularly between the bottom half of the First Division and the top half of the Second, only went and defied the mind-boggling 5000/1 odds and created one of the greatest sporting fairy tales of all time. The story, however, was to have the saddest of postscripts.

Claudio Ranieri, the manager of Leicester when they unexpectedly won the Premier League title in 2015/16, summed up the man perfectly in five words: "Everything he touched became better."

Foreign owners are often viewed with suspicion in English football and with good reason. Many don't truly 'get' what it's all about and leave with stinging criticisms from fans. Khun Vichai was certainly different. He went about his business fairly quietly after buying Leicester in 2010, rarely giving interviews and having trust in the managers he hired and players he bought to try and deliver the kind of success he'd already had in other areas of his life.

It was never about him. He let others take the glory. Make no mistake, though – he was the chief architect of the rise and rise of a football club which had endured a number of difficult years, being on the brink of liquidation and even sliding into the third tier for the only time in their history. Vichai certainly had dreams and he fulfilled those for supporters too.

After play-off heartbreak at Watford, the Foxes romped to the Championship title. A year later, they were seemingly doomed to relegation until the greatest of great escapes saved them. The mega-rich elite didn't know what had hit them the following year as the no-hopers ripped up the formbook. Champions League quarter finalists in 2017? Yeah, they managed that as well.

There were so many reasons to love Vichai. Not just the impact he had with results on the pitch but how he treated fans as supporters rather than just customers. He'd give away season tickets, scarves, beer, cakes and much more. He didn't have to. He wanted to. To fans, it felt like he was the head of their football family and that family feeling was certainly important to him.

To the wider public he was also appreciated as donations were made to hospitals and charities. Not just a few quid here and there. We're talking millions. None of this, you felt, was done to see his name surrounded by flashing lights. He just wanted to make a difference. The outpouring of grief following his death showed how greatly that difference was felt.

So many stories emerged after the tragedy of the things he'd done to make the lives of other people better. Some were small but meant a huge amount to those involved. He'd stop and chat with fans, have selfies. You didn't hear people say bad words about him which is unusual in this modern age of social media anger.

He was humble despite his successful business empire and huge wealth. When he did speak, he came across as someone who just wanted to enjoy life. "I feel very fortunate because I do what I love," he said in 2016, "so I put love into everything I do."

As a local lad, I've watched Leicester since 1981 and reported on them as a journalist since 1989. The club has never had an owner like him. Like most in the media, I didn't know him personally. He would say hello and shake hands on the few occasions our paths would cross. With what he'd achieved in life he commanded respect. He never sought it, but he certainly earned it.

Many scoffed when he said he would take Leicester into Europe. He believed. That belief rubbed off on managers, players and fans. He took us on a magnificent journey and helped write a story which will be talked about for many generations. It will seem utterly mad in decades to come to reflect on such a brief but incredible period.

The day Leicester lifted the Premier League trophy in May 2016 was an 'I was there' moment. Bright sunshine accompanied a spine-tingling performance from operatic legend Andrea Bocelli. The rain mercilessly lashed down during the game with Everton and then, right on cue, with the post-match celebrations due to start, the weather changed again. Golden rays from above lit up the King Power Stadium. A rainbow brought more colour from the sky. It was that kind of season.

At the same venue, in October 2018, the tears of joy and celebration were replaced by those of utter sadness and pain. From the highest high to the lowest low. The helicopter rose from the centre of the pitch, as it always did, but this time there was a major problem. Within moments a nightmare unfolded. None of us there that night will forget the things we saw, as much as we try. Fans gathered, shocked and numb. The tributes began. And they kept on coming. Supporters shared their collective grief. Players were in tears, rocked to the core. He was their friend as well as 'The Boss'.

The story of Khun Vichai's love and generosity was brought to a wider audience. He touched the lives of so many. He leaves a legacy that will always be talked about in the most glowing terms. He dreamed the impossible dream and turned it into reality. He gave Leicester fans the most incredible memories and allowed supporters of other clubs to feel they too could achieve great things.

He became one of our own.
His song will never end.

Geoff Peters
@mrgeoffpeters
April 2019

Introduction

Introduction

In 2012, Bangkok-born businessman Vichai Raksriaksorn and his family were bestowed with a new surname by the late King of Thailand, Bhumibol Adulyadej. The gifted 'Srivaddhanaprabha' title –roughly translates as "light of progressive glory". It seems appropriate given Khun Vichai's ability to illuminate hope and success on those who featured in his rich life tapestry.

Nowhere were Vichai's radiating qualities felt more so than in Leicester – a city situated in the East Midlands of England with a population of around 350,000. Before the arrival of the Thai duty-free magnate at the local football club, the city was perhaps best known as the home of the Walkers snack food brand, the birthplace of BBC *Match of the Day* presenter Gary Lineker and, more latterly, as the resting place of King Richard III.

All that changed in May 2016, when the city was thrust into the global spotlight with Leicester City Football Club having completed the most unlikely of football fairy tales. Under Vichai's chairmanship and the management of popular Italian Claudio Ranieri, the Foxes smashed odds of 5000-1 at the start of the 2015/16 campaign to win that season's Premier League title.

The triumph will be remembered for many things. The saves from goalkeeper Kasper Schmeichel and the central defensive solidity of Wes Morgan and Robert Huth. The remarkable Premier League debut season of N'Golo Kante and the individual brilliance of Riyad Mahrez, not to mention the goals of Jamie Vardy. But behind the scenes at the King Power Stadium – so named after Vichai's company King Power International Group – the Thai owner, had his own unique role in English football's biggest-ever surprise success story.

As Vichai made the impossible become possible on the pitch, he had the exact same impact in the local community. The tales of the charities he supported and the individuals he helped have become as much a part of Leicester folklore as the achievements of the 'fearless' Foxes.

While even the most optimistic Leicester City fan would acknowledge that being crowned champions of England was true, once-in-a-lifetime stuff, they could still dare to dream big after that triumph. Administration had been the club's reality back in 2002 but the Thai cleared their debts and regularly allowed them to compete for and sign players priced in excess of £20m. From playing in the third tier of the Football League in 2008/09, Leicester reached the quarter finals of the UEFA Champions League just seven years after his arrival.

At the start of the 2018/19 campaign, a new £100m training ground and a stadium expansion were on the horizon while a regular place in the richest league in the world looked assured. All this for a set of supporters once used to Leicester City being one of English football's classic yo-yo clubs.

His £2m gift to Leicester Hospitals Charity and £1m donation to the University of Leicester's medical department meant bright things lay ahead for some of the city's most important institutions too. And in his native Thailand, many charitable initiatives he established continued to prosper while his aim of King Power becoming the world's "leading travel retailer" carried with it the prospect of new jobs.

Vichai Srivaddhanaprabha looked set to continue to be the man who made dreams a reality...

Chapter One

The Darkest Hour

After heading a consortium that purchased Leicester City Football Club back in August 2010, the sight of club owner Vichai Srivaddhanaprabha departing the Foxes' King Power Stadium in a helicopter became commonplace on a matchday. His latest model – a 2016 AgustaWestland AW169 – had a blue and white livery, inspired by the colours of both Leicester City and his travel retail company, King Power International Group. It also carried a Foxes crest.

"Helicopter travel was a necessity for a businessman as active as Leicester City owner Vichai Srivaddhanaprabha," read a *Leicester Mercury* article, profiling the club chairman's life. "With a business empire in Asia and interests in London and Leicester, flying became the most effective way to travel for the club's owner as he could be back in the capital in around 30 minutes."

Despite his busy lifestyle, Khun Vichai attended the majority of Leicester City home matches and on October 27, 2018 he headed off on another pilgrimage to his beloved club for their Premier League clash with West Ham United. With the fixture broadcast on BT Sport in the United Kingdom, the Thai headed off slightly later than usual for a Saturday match, with a 5:30pm kick-off time.

His helicopter – registration G-VSKP, with the initials presumably standing for 'Vichai Srivaddhanaprabha, King Power' – departed Fairoaks Airport in Surrey that afternoon. It stopped at London Helipad – close to Vichai's home in Chelsea Wharf – to pick up the Foxes chairman plus two of his staff before departing at 2:43pm. It subsequently arrived at Leicester City's training complex on Belvoir Drive at 3:48pm, with the passengers disembarking and taking the remaining 1.5-mile journey to the King Power Stadium by car.

Having fallen behind to a 30th minute goal from West Ham's Fabian Balbuena, Leicester's hopes of getting back into the match looked to have been bolstered eight minutes later when the Hammers' Mark Noble was sent-off. Goalkeeper Lukasz Fabianski frustrated the Foxes with a string of excellent saves before Wilfred Ndidi equalised for the home side with a minute of normal time remaining. His long-range strike deflected off Balbuena to wrong-foot Fabianski.

After the match, watched by a crowd of 31,848, pilot Eric Swaffer – along with his girlfriend and co-pilot Izabela Roza Lechowicz – headed to the club's training ground by car to collect the helicopter. He flew it to the King Power Stadium to pick-up Vichai and two members of his staff, Kaveporn Punpare and Nusara Suknamai. The flight was bound for London Stanstead Airport.

At approximately 8:37pm, the helicopter began to take off from within the stadium. The BT Sport cameras were rolling at that time, filming the *Premier League Tonight* show. Host Jake Humphrey and studio guests Owen Hargreaves, Chris Sutton and John Hartson looked out of their studio window at the ground as the rotor blades whirred. Humphrey made an admiring remark about Vichai's mode of transport while Hartson joked that Sutton's "fee for today" was on board.

It was a rare moment of humour on a difficult day for BT Sport and the football community as a whole, which had begun with Glenn Hoddle collapsing off-air while appearing on the broadcaster's *Saturday Morning Savage* show. It subsequently transpired that the former England player and manager had suffered a heart attack, from which he fortunately made a full recovery. Elsewhere that afternoon, a Brighton & Hove Albion supporter died having been taken ill before the Seagulls' Premier League match against Wolverhampton Wanderers.

Alas, Humphrey would soon have to report on another shocking news story. This time, one that occurred just a few hundred yards away from his studio.

Seconds after take-off, Vichai's helicopter began to spin uncontrollably, with the Air Accidents Investigation Branch's (AAIB) Bulletin S1/2018 later reporting that it "reached a radio height of approximately 430ft before descending with a high rotation rate."

"The helicopter struck the ground in an approximately upright position on a stepped concrete surface, with the landing gear retracted, and rolled onto its left side," continued the AAIB Bulletin. "The helicopter was rapidly engulfed in an intense post-impact fire. Stadium staff and emergency services were quickly at the scene but were not able to gain access to the helicopter because of the intensity of the fire."

As Humphrey and co discussed the topic of AFC Bournemouth manager Eddie Howe "being considered for one of the top jobs in English football" on the *Premier League Tonight* show, the muffled sound of the helicopter's impact in the stadium Car Park E could be heard. During the commercial break, details of what had happened reached the studio.

"Things have taken a very sad turn in the last few moments," a visibly shaken Humphrey told BT Sport viewers. "Obviously it's been a very difficult day already because we had the news this morning that our great friend and colleague Glenn Hoddle was taken ill.

"We've just seen the Leicester City owner's helicopter take off from the centre circle here at Leicester City. It's something that is a very regular feature for us. We often sit here after the games and see the helicopter take off, make remarks about owning a football club and flying in a helicopter.

"However, it's suddenly got very serious because the helicopter that took off from here just about five minutes ago whilst we were live on air... has crashed. It's crashed in the club car park just outside the window here. We were on air, we heard a commotion. No news on casualties, no news on who was in the helicopter, nothing's been confirmed."

Having just finished recording his post-match interviews for Sky Sports News, cameraman Dan Cox was walking across one of the stadium's car parks.

"I heard the helicopter coming out of the stadium, saw it as you do, they are amazing pieces of machinery and then I just carried on walking thinking next time I look up it is going to be overhead," Cox told Sky News. "The next thing I just looked up and it was just spinning, static just out of control, just a constant spinning, I have never seen anything like it."

As news of the helicopter crash emerged, Leicestershire Police released a short statement, which read; "We are dealing with an incident in the vicinity of the King Power Stadium. Emergency services are aware and dealing." Leicester City Football Club also released a brief statement on the night of the crash, which added; "We are assisting Leicestershire Police and the Emergency Services in dealing with a major incident at King Power Stadium. The Club will issue a more detailed statement once further information has been established."

It wasn't until late evening the following day that the devastating news of the death of Vichai and the four other people on-board the helicopter was made public. In between that time, a collective shock and numbness gripped the football world.

"The 24 hours after the crash were probably the worst, because nothing was official in terms of who was in the helicopter," remembered Foxes Trust Chairman Ian Bason. "On the day the crash happened, I remember the helicopter approaching the stadium just as I was getting into my car to leave. I didn't notice anything unusual and I was listening to BBC Radio Leicester when it landed. Shortly after I arrived home, I got a phone call from the vice-chairman of the Trust, who informed me about what had happened."

With the events of October 27, 2018, the day's football action paled into insignificance. Gary Lineker, who was born in Leicester on November 30, 1960 and started his playing career with his home city club, reflected the sombre mood and concerns of everyone as the BBC's *Match of the Day* show began that evening.

"Hello, we'd normally come on air and tell you about the games to look forward to seeing in the show... This, though, is no ordinary Saturday," he started. "First, everyone at *Match of the Day* sends our best wishes to Glenn Hoddle who collapsed while working for BT Sport. Glenn was transferred to a hospital in London and his condition is described as serious. But we're told he is currently receiving specialist treatment and responding well. His family have thanked everyone for their support and our thoughts are with them and with Glenn.

"Then, after Leicester played West Ham the helicopter owned by the owner, Vichai Srivaddhanaprabha, crashed outside the ground. Clearly, this is a breaking story. We'll do our best to keep you updated through the programme."

Lineker later took to Twitter to describe that Saturday night's edition of *Match of the Day* as the toughest he had ever presented. "Thoughts are with everyone at Leicester City. A terrible tragedy. Heartbreaking," he tweeted.

The morning after the most shocking night before began for many by tuning into television and radio for further news of Hoddle's condition and more details of what had happened in Leicester. By this stage, people had started to arrive at the King Power Stadium to lay flowers, football shirts and scarves in tribute to those on-board the helicopter, while large images of both Vichai and the Hindu god Ganesh were put on display.

"Watching all the tributes, seeing children putting things down at the stadium... it was all very upsetting and moving," remembered Bason. "We were seeing fellow fans we knew well but also fans who had never been to a match but felt compelled to come to the stadium and of course supporters of other clubs who wanted to pay their respects."

In the aftermath of the crash, there were inaccurate suggestions in some sections of the media that Vichai's daughter Voramas had been on board the helicopter. Thankfully, that speculation proved to be unfounded. Hours after the incident, Sky Sports News reported that, according to their sources, neither Vice-Chairman Aiyawatt Srivaddhanaprabha nor Director of Football Jon Rudkin were part of the travelling party. Monaco coach Gregory Campi – a close friend of then-Foxes Manager Claude Puel – confirmed in the French newspaper *Nice Matin* that Puel was safe. "I spoke to him last night. Claude and his wife are fine," said Campi.

It was around 10pm on October 28, 2018 that the news of those who had passed away was made public. Leicester City confirmed the death of their chairman and four other people in a statement that read;

"It is with the deepest regret and a collective broken heart that we confirm our Chairman, Vichai Srivaddhanaprabha, was among those to have tragically lost their lives on Saturday evening when a helicopter carrying him and four other people crashed outside King Power Stadium. None of the five people on-board survived.

"The primary thoughts of everyone at the Club are with the Srivaddhanaprabha family and the families of all those on-board at this time of unspeakable loss.

"In Khun Vichai, the world has lost a great man. A man of kindness, of generosity and a man whose life was defined by the love he devoted to his family and those he so successfully led. Leicester City was a family under his leadership. It is as a family that we will grieve his passing and maintain the pursuit of a vision for the Club that is now his legacy."

Leicestershire Police meanwhile named the five individuals believed to have died in a separate statement. "While formal identification has not yet taken place, they are believed to be Leicester City Football Club Chairman Vichai Srivaddhanaprabha, two members of his staff, Nusara Suknamai and Kaveporn Punpare, pilot Eric Swaffer and passenger Izabela Roza Lechowicz," it read. "The force has been working to ensure that all the relevant next of kin had been informed prior to this information being confirmed publicly."

Understandably, in light of what happened, Leicester City confirmed in their statement that their matches scheduled for Tuesday 30 October, 2018 – a first-team fixture against Southampton in the EFL Cup and the Development Squad clash against Feyenoord in the Premier League International Cup – had been postponed.

While much of the focus around the tragedy was on the death of Vichai, further details of the other four victims began to emerge.

Eric Swaffer, 43, had over 20 years' flying experience as a private jet and helicopter pilot. He flew helicopters for live media broadcasting during his career including Channel 4's *The Big Breakfast* and Virgin Radio, while he was also a Joint Aviation Authority (JAA) instructor and examiner for several aircraft and helicopter types. His career had taken him all around the world and he met a number of influential figures along the way, including the Dalai Lama.

Swaffer has been hailed as a hero for steering the helicopter – which was subsequently found to have a broken tail rotor control linkage – away from the stadium and other busy parts of the surrounding area. Sky Sports News photographer Dan Cox told *The Mirror* newspaper, "He [Swaffer] managed to crash that helicopter in a part of the ground where there wasn't anybody there. The pilot was heroic and the two police officers in front of me, who also tried to help, they are heroes too."

More than 1,000 staff, corporate guests and members of the media were known to have still been inside the ground at the time of the crash.

Speaking to BBC Radio 5 Live after Swaffer's death, long-time friend Lucie Morris-Marr paid tribute to the heroic pilot. "Having been lucky to have known him as a friend and flown with him a few times as a passenger, it doesn't surprise me that he would have done all he could to save lives and do everything in his power to avoid a worse outcome in those final moments," she said. "He was an incredible person and very focused when flying."

Morris-Marr described Swaffer as "extremely funny, charming and cheeky with a wicked sense of humour" and added; "everyone loved him. I'm not surprised the chairman hired him. He was always great company."

Swaffer died that tragic night alongside 46-year-old girlfriend Izabela Roza Lechowicz. A fellow pilot, Lechowicz moved from Poland to the United Kingdom in 1997. At the start of 2018, she was included in a project called 'Polka100', that celebrated women getting the vote in Poland in 1918. She was selected by the country's embassy as a Polish woman that inspired the community in the UK because of her chosen vocation.

Swaffer and Lechowicz had been partners for around ten years prior to the crash and had recently bought a home together in Camberley, Surrey. In her interview with BBC Radio 5 Live, their friend Lucie Morris-Marr, dubbed their romance as an "aviation love story".

"Not many people get to work and travel with their soulmate, travelling the world going to glamorous places," commented Morris-Marr.

Born on May 6, 1985 in Pathum Thani in Thailand, Nusara Suknamai was Vichai's personal assistant. The 32-year-old, who was a runner-up in Thailand's *Miss Universe* contest in 2005, regularly attended Leicester matches following Vichai's purchase of the club. There were numerous photographs of her with Foxes players on her Instagram page, which also showed her attending the 2018 FIFA World Cup in Russia. There is a humorous video of her on social media attempting the so-called 'Dele Alli Challenge' with former England international Jamie Vardy.

Fellow Thai Kaveporn Punpare was the last victim of the helicopter crash to be formally identified. The 33-year-old from Bangkok was understood to be another member of Vichai's staff. Less is known about Punpare than the other four passengers. His Facebook account shows photographs of him travelling around the world, with snaps in Paris, Moscow and London while there are a number of images of him at Old Trafford, the home of Manchester United Football Club.

Following the announcement five people had lost their lives, an investigation into the cause of the crash began. "The AAIB is now leading an investigation to establish the exact circumstances surrounding the crash and investigators will remain at the scene to complete their initial enquiries," confirmed Leicestershire Police Superintendent Steve Potter at the time.

"It is likely to take several days to fully complete the necessary work and to safely deal with the scene of this tragic accident, during that time we ask that both the media and public resist speculating around the cause of the crash.

"Our thoughts today are with the families of those who have sadly died, with Leicester City Football Club, and with both football supporters and the wider local community who have all been impacted by the events of last night and the news that those on board the aircraft have not survived."

Chapter Two

Starting Out

Throughout his life, Vichai Srivaddhanaprabha kept a distinctly low profile. In his capacity as Leicester City owner and chairman, he never engaged with the British media beyond mere pleasantries and he was seldom interviewed back home in Thailand either, despite the rise-and-rise of his football club and duty-free empire, King Power.

Such was Vichai's willingness to steer clear of the limelight, even some of the most basic details about his life remain a mystery. It is regularly reported that he was born in Bangkok on April 4, 1958 – with Leicester City always celebrating his birthday around that date. But other sources – including the Companies House AP01 'Appointment of Director' form he signed during his takeover of the Foxes in 2010 – cite his date of birth as being June 5, 1958.

There is very little information in the public domain regarding Vichai's upbringing either. Born as 'Vichai Raksriaksorn' to a Thai-Chinese family, his parents Wiwat and Prapasorn Raksriaksorn are understood to have been of relatively modest means. According to *The Nation* – one of Thailand's leading English-language newspapers – he was educated in the United States of America, attending 'Woodlawn High School'. Alas, despite contacting a series of schools as part of the research for this book, it is still not known which 'Woodlawn High' the newspaper is referring to.

The Nation also claimed that Vichai obtained a bachelor's degree from the Faculty of Liberal Arts at Ramkhamhaeng University while he also completed a degree course at Northrop University's Business Administration Faculty in the United States. The latter organisation, based in Inglewood, California, closed its doors in 1993. It has also been suggested that he studied in Taiwan for a period.

There is conjecture too regarding Vichai's journey in the business world. In an article for Reuters, Patpicha Tanakasempipat suggests he very much worked his way up as he "rose from obscurity as a printer and leather goods trader" prior to establishing King Power International Group in 1989. Other sources give an impression of a man that found himself in senior roles from an early age. "He became a vastly experienced businessman, both from his own and jointly-managed companies, including Sriaksorn (1980), Thai Nishikawa International, Europa Prince (Thailand), and Downtown DFS (Thailand)," wrote The Nation.

The same publication claims that he made his initial breakthrough into the travel retail industry in Hong Kong, prior to returning to his native Thailand. King Power was founded on the back of Vichai being granted a licence to operate the country's first downtown duty-free shop at Bangkok's Mahatun Plaza. The store opened its doors for the first time on October 18, 1989, initially trading as 'TAT Duty Free'.

King Power's expansion was rapid. In 1991, the organisation received its first overseas licence to set up the 'Khmer Duty Free' shop at Cambodia's Phnom Penh International Airport. This was quickly followed with permission to open a merchandise store at Don Mueang – then Bangkok's main airport – which was granted in 1993. Two years later, King Power won the sole concession to operate at Don Mueang, while former Thai Prime Minister Chavalit Yongchaiyudh awarded the company with a ten-year contract to manage – exclusively – the duty-free business at the World Trade Centre in downtown Bangkok.

Within its first ten years of trading, King Power opened a shop alongside the Great Wall of China as well as further duty-free stores at Chiang Mai, Hat Yai and Phuket international airports. The company was also given the rights to manage an in-flight duty-free operation on board Thai Airways flights.

Only those in Vichai's inner-circle know the details of how he met his wife Aimon, where and when they got married etc. Their first child, Voramas – also known as 'Rux', was born in Bangkok in 1981. She attended a boarding school in England prior to enrolling on a degree course in textile design at Chelsea College of Arts and went on to complete a master's degree in Fashion Accessories at Central Saint Martins. Voramas eventually began working for her father's company as a merchandiser and was heavily involved in the organisation, setting up their retail operation at Suvarnabhumi International Airport. She has also appeared as the face of some of the organisation's advertising campaigns. In her current role as Executive Vice President of Group Marketing, she oversees King Power's marketing strategy and corporate communications.

Voramas' brother Apichet was born around a year later and also attended an English boarding school before obtaining a degree in the Science of Marketing with Psychology. He currently holds the position of Assistant to Group Chairman at King Power and was appointed to the Leicester City board in August 2014. Nicknamed 'Tip' or 'Tal', Apichet is an outstanding polo player, as is his younger brother Aiyawatt or 'Top', who was born on July 26, 1985. The pair have represented Thailand in the sport at international level and are key players in King Power's High Goal teams.

Top was educated at Saint Gabriel's College – a private Catholic all-boys school in Bangkok – and obtained a Bachelor of Business Administration degree from the Bangkok University International Program. Prior to the death of his father, he had risen to the position of CEO and vice-chairman of King Power, while he also held senior executive and administrative capacities at numerous associated companies, including holding the vice-chairman position at Leicester City Football Club.

It was Top who started the Srivaddhanaprabha love affair with Leicester City, having travelled to one of the club's matches as a youngster. He was a regular at the King Power Stadium and was usually on board his father's helicopter after home fixtures. Thankfully, fate would decree that Top would be elsewhere on October 27, 2018. In the years leading up to the tragedy he had been spending more time in Thailand due to his senior role at King Power and that is where he was on that terrible night.

Like his father, Top is a devoted Buddhist and was ordained as a monk at the Thepsirin Buddhist Temple in Bangkok in 2015. A year earlier, he was awarded an honorary doctorate by De Montfort University for his work in business and the contribution he made to the Leicester community. Vichai and Aimon's other child Aroonroong is also an executive at King Power, working as an Assistant to the Chief Financial Officer. According to a number of media outlets, each of the Srivaddhanaprabha children were allocated a 10% stake in Leicester City prior to Vichai's death while Aimon holds a 9% share. It is understood that most of the family's King Power shares are held through the Thailand-based V&A Holdings.

Way before his purchase of Leicester City Football Club, Vichai was a committed Anglophile. As King Power grew during the mid-1990s, it is understood he bought his first home in the United Kingdom with a close friend of his citing the country's appeals to the Thai magnate. "England is the centre of society and polo in Europe... one of Vichai's great passions. The fact he also spoke English meant many factors were perfect for him to buy a property there," said Oliver Winter, President of the German Polo Association.

It is believed Vichai's first British home was in Berkshire – a county he maintained strong links with thereafter. He established the King Power Foxes polo club at Gadbridge Farm on Forest Green Road in Holyport – a village close to Maidenhead – in 2014. While three of his children were educated in England, it wasn't until around 2002 that the businessman started to spend a considerable amount of time in the United Kingdom, having been based in Thailand for the majority of his working life. Early into the new millennium, it is understood that he bought his second British property in London.

A defining year in Vichai's life came in 2006, when then-Thai Prime Minister Thaksin Shinawatra – a former telecoms tycoon and Manchester City owner – awarded King Power with an exclusive duty-free contract at the new Suvarnabhumi International Airport in Bangkok. Suvarnabhumi, which opened on September 28, 2006, has established itself as one of the world's busiest airports and is Thailand's main hub for international flights.

The extent of King Power's monopoly at the airport was reflected in Issue 22 of the *Moodie Report*. Published in October 2006, the travel-retail publication reported from Suvarnabhumi's opening.

"King Power holds separate ten-year concessions for the duty-free and other commercial facilities. Besides 19 duty-free stores covering 10,000sqm, King Power has had to design and build some 297 commercial retail units, embracing food and beverage, entertainment and services, spread over 27,500sqm of space… The main duty-free zones comprise a 999m walkway, said to be the longest in the world.

"King Power signs are prominent throughout the landside departures area, building passenger interest in what lies airside. There's even a luxury Bentley motor vehicle in place, advertising a King Power and Visa Card promotion offering the chance to win the car or your weight in gold – one chance for every 5,000 (Thai Baht) or $130 (US Dollar) spent."

A notable store within the airport at its opening was 'VR' – which carried Vichai's former initials. The boutique stocked the King Power chairman's own lifestyle fashion brand and accessories while the adjacent 'Memories of Thailand' concession sold floral bracelets in return for a $1 donation to world poverty relief programmes – an early example of the philanthropy that Vichai became so renowned for.

2006 also saw the opening of King Power's 'Downtown Complex' on Rangnam Road in central Bangkok, which opened six weeks prior to Suvarnabhumi. The $134m retail mall incorporates 10,650sqm of shopping space over three floors as well as a 600-seat restaurant and offices. A hotel and theatre were later constructed on the same site.

King Power and Vichai's rise from that point was dramatic. In 2007, Raksriaksorn was ranked 21st in Forbes's list of Thailand's wealthiest, worth an estimated $200m (£141m). Less than a decade later, he had risen to fourth with an estimated fortune of $2.8bn. After its first two decades of operation, King Power estimated its turnover at 128bn ($3.8bn).

The growth of King Power continued throughout 2007, as a new concession was secured to manage an in-flight duty-free operation on board Thai Airways aircrafts, with similar contracts agreed with AirAsia in 2011 and Thai AirAsia X in 2014. In August 2010, Vichai headed a consortium called Asia Football Investments that purchased then-Championship club Leicester City for an estimated £39m. A week before purchasing the club, King Power agreed a sponsorship deal with the Foxes that saw their name splashed on the front of its shirts. Its stadium was named after the company a year later, increasing knowledge of King Power outside of Asia.

While Vichai and his family never took a penny out of Leicester City, other than relatively minimal management fees and other related costs, there is no doubt they used the club to help bolster King Power's appeal. Particularly after the club's Premier League triumph in 2015, it was almost impossible to go through a Thai airport without seeing an image of the Foxes and the company together. A video advert showed striker Jamie Vardy purchasing gifts at one of their duty-free stores, while King Power also sold collectable gift cards of the team which became sought-after items in Thailand. The club's official replica kit has even sold out in the country on a few occasions.

Towards the end of 2010, King Power was conferred a royal warrant from the King of Thailand – becoming one of only 41 companies in the country ever to receive the prestigious recognition. A garuda statue – a legendary bird-like creature in

Buddhist mythology – stands at the front of the organisation's headquarters in Bangkok to symbolise that privilege. Vichai and his family received another major honour from the King of Thailand, Bhumibol Adulyadej in 2012 when they were bestowed with the 'Srivaddhanaprabha' surname.

Away from royalty, there have been regular nods to King Power from within the travel-retail industry. It became the first organisation to win both 'Best Airport Retailer' and 'Best Land-Based Border/Downtown Retailer' titles at the Frontier Awards in Cannes in 2011. That same year, the group was granted a licence to open Thailand's first regional duty-free store in the eastern region, with the King Power Complex at the popular coastal resort of Pattaya. Around that time, King Power revisited some of its early history by setting up a new duty-free shop at Don Mueang Airport, which had reopened following a major renovation.

One of King Power's most eye-catching developments is their Srivaree Complex – situated a short distance from Suvarnabhumi airport to the east of Bangkok. Opened in 2013, the two-storey, duty-free outlet has a striking architectural design, with a gold criss-cross pattern taking influence from local handicrafts. The on-site Ramayana restaurant serves an international buffet and can accommodate up to 1,500 visitors.

King Power's relationship with Leicester City was celebrated in 2014, as the organisation opened the first official Foxes fan store in Thailand, situated at BTS Siam railway station. Further club concessions have since been added at Suvarnabhumi and Phuket airports as well as King Power's complex in downtown Bangkok.

By the latter years of Vichai's life, King Power's investments had become notably diverse. Having already purchased a substantial stake in Accor's Pullman hotels in Thailand, they purchased a $226m stake in Thai AirAsia – the country's largest budget airline – in June 2016. The 39% ownership of holding company Asia Aviation (AAV) made King Power the second largest shareholder in Thai AirAsia. At the time of the purchase, Agence France-Presse reported that King Power had ambitions to buy the remaining 61% of the company but in 2017, they sold 36.3% of their stake in AAV to Thai AirAsia's CEO Tassapon Bijleveld.

Vichai and King Power purchased their second football club – Belgian second-tier side Oud-Heverlee Leuven – in May 2017. By the end of the year, the company's profits soared to a record level of $2.141bn, with some 7,000 employees working for the organisation by that stage. King Power's profitability, driven mainly by its duty-free empire at Thailand's airports, was emphasised in an article by Bloomberg in 2018.

"In the first nine months of 2018, almost 80 million passengers came through Suvarnabhumi and the capital's second airport, Don Mueang, another King Power concession," it read. "While tourism growth has spluttered recently, the sector remains a key engine of Southeast Asia's second-largest economy."

At the start of 2018, King Power reopened its Rangnam complex in downtown Bangkok, which had been the subject of a major refurbishment and expansion, said to have cost some $74m. Speaking to the *Moodie Davitt Report*, Vichai's son Aiyawatt hailed the outlet as "one of Bangkok's major landmarks" and added; "King Power Rangnam is a symbol of thriving tourism in Thailand and the industry's importance to its people and our economy. It is where world class brands are continually introduced to Thailand and where Thai products are given a gateway to the global marketplace."

A few months later, King Power completed the purchase of the spectacular 314-metre MahaNakhon skyscraper in the Bang Rak district of Bangkok which was subsequently renamed King Power MahaNakhon. The mixed-use complex – designed by Ole Scheeren and developed by PACE Development – has 78 floors and was previously Thailand's tallest building prior to the opening of Magnolias Waterfront Residences at ICONSIAM in 2018. The tower incorporates a 154-room hotel, residential properties, restaurants, public observation points as well as 10,000sqm of retail space. The Bt21b ($620m) development has 209 residences serviced by Ritz-Carlton which are said to be amongst the most expensive luxury real estate in the country.

King Power's purchase of the MahaNakhon saw Vichai dubbed the 'Master of the Big Deal' in an article in *The Nation* newspaper, pointing out that he had "bagged many big deals in Thailand's business history."

By the time of his death in October 2018, Vichai was said to be worth around $5bn by Forbes. During his life, the Thai mogul enjoyed the trappings of his success. One of his most lavish purchases was a Gulfstream G650 business jet, which *BizJet Blogger* claimed he paid $72m for to Fabiana Flosi – the wife of Bernie Ecclestone – in 2013. He also splashed out on a 116ft superyacht – worth an estimated £11m – and had a penchant for £200 bottles of Saint-Émilion Grand Cru according to a *MailOnline* article. Vichai employed around 60 staff and stabled approximately 80 horses on his 100-acre estate in Berkshire, while his London property overlooked a picturesque park on the banks of the River Thames.

As *The Independent* pointed out in their obituary to the 60-year-old, Vichai was "no ordinary [football] club owner" and neither, it seems, was he any 'ordinary' billionaire either. While he clearly enjoyed the 'high life', it seemed happiness rather than wealth and material possessions was his greatest motivation. After he was awarded an honorary degree by the University of Leicester he gave an insight into his life and business ethos. "I feel very fortunate because I do what I love," he said, "so I put love into everything I do."

Chapter Three

The Beautiful Game

On April 6, 1997, Vichai's then 11-year-old son Aiyawatt attended his first-ever football match in England – the Football League Cup Final between Leicester City and Middlesbrough at the original Wembley Stadium. For whatever reason – perhaps swayed by the Foxes' blue and white kit, which matched the corporate colours of his father's business, King Power – 'Top' decided to cheer on Leicester that afternoon.

Having fallen behind in extra-time to a strike from Italian forward Fabrizio Ravanelli, the Foxes battled back to salvage a draw two minutes before the final whistle, as Emile Heskey equalised for Martin O'Neill's team. Ten days later, Leicester beat Middlesbrough 1-0 after extra-time in the replay at Hillsborough to lift the League Cup for the second time in their history.

Top instantly fell in love with Leicester City and that final ended up being a glorious one for the Foxes in more than one way. Aside from yielding a major piece of silverware at the time, it also proved the long-term catalyst for Vichai to purchase the club.

"He [Top] told me the reason he decided Leicester was the club he'd like his father to invest in was that as a football-mad youngster he had travelled to England to watch a game in 1997," wrote BBC Radio Leicester journalist Ian Stringer.

Polo was Vichai's first sporting passion but he had a long-established interest in football too. Unsurprisingly for a devoted Anglophile, his favourite competition was the Premier League.

In the early 2000s, he started attending Chelsea matches at Stamford Bridge – the West Londoners' blue kit doubtlessly appealing to the businessman, as was the club's proximity to his London home. He was likely to have been living in SW6 by that period in his life. He eventually purchased an executive suite there, apparently choosing hospitality box number eight in the West Stand because of the Chinese tradition of that being a lucky number.

In a Thai language book called *The Fairy Tale of Underfox* by Bell Jiradet – which covers King Power's time at Leicester City and features an exclusive interview with Top – there is a story of how Vichai's interest in Chelsea later waned. The Raksriaksorn family were understood to have attended a UEFA Champions League tie at Stamford Bridge in 2006, when there was some kind of issue with security staff which resulted in Vichai almost accidentally being hit in the face with a metal detector. According to the book, the King Power owner vowed never to return to the club as a Blues supporter and told Top "Someday, we will buy a football team that can compete with Chelsea!"

The *Reading Chronicle* wrote that Vichai apparently approached Reading Football Club regarding a potential takeover back in 2007, but a deal was never struck. It is also understood he made similar enquiries with other clubs before establishing a relationship with Leicester City. Just a week after King Power agreed a three-year shirt sponsorship with the Foxes, a consortium led by Vichai agreed to purchase the club for a fee of £39m from former Portsmouth owner Milan Mandaric, who stayed on as club chairman for a brief period.

In a rare interview with the *Sunday Times*, Vichai briefly explained his decision to buy Leicester City in August 2010, who were a Football League Championship club at that time.

"After spending time studying many clubs, I fell in love with Leicester," he said. "One reason was the colours, which were the same as my company's. The other was the fact they were playing in the second tier. If we bought a Premier League club, it wouldn't be challenging enough."

Three years after purchasing Leicester City, Vichai converted the club's £103m debt into shares. The act both "wiped out the club's liabilities and forfeited his ability to call in the money in one swoop," wrote the financial publication *City AM*. His actions demonstrated the club was a long-term project – in vast contrast to compatriot Thaksin Shinawatra, who bought Manchester City in 2007 and sold just a year later for a £20m profit. In an interview with AFP, Vichai stated: "I've never had an idea to work with the team for a short period and then sell it," he said.

Prior to Vichai's arrival at Leicester City, the club had been blighted by financial problems. The lowest point for the Foxes came in October 2002, when they were plunged into administration with a reported debt of £30m. Saviour came in the shape of a consortium led by former player Gary Lineker, who took the club out of administration – aided by funds from the Leicester City Supporters' Trust, now known as the Foxes Trust.

"We managed to save the club with an investment of £6.5m as a consortium, but the feeling in the years that followed was that we weren't really progressing as a football club," said Ian Bason, Chairman of the Foxes Trust.

In February 2007, the club was sold again to Milan Mandaric, who endured a torrid introduction to life at Leicester City. After sacking manager Rob Kelly shortly after becoming chairman, he saw his next managerial appointment, Martin Allen, depart after just three months. Gary Megson's exit was even swifter – leaving to manage Bolton Wanderers after only six weeks with the Foxes.

"Milan promised to take us out of the Championship," lamented Bason. "He achieved that... taking us into League One! We should have clarified what he meant!

"The Trust never had the best relationship with Milan. I think that goes back to the fact we were very questioning of him when he first took over the club. That started the relationship off on a slightly tricky wicket. It wasn't the case that we couldn't work with him, more that he was pretty guarded. One of the things we asked him – which seems surreal to talk about given what happened to Vichai – was what would happen in the event that he passed away while he was Leicester City chairman. That question was never really addressed and that concerned us."

After Leicester's relegation to the third-tier of English football for the first time in 2008, the Foxes made an instant return to the Championship by winning the League One title in 2008/09. Prior to King Power's purchase, the club had shown promising form by finishing fifth in the division in 2009/10 and reaching the play-offs.

Given the rollercoaster ride Leicester City endured during the 2000s, it's fair to say the club's supporters were somewhat guarded ahead of the arrival of Vichai's 'Asian Football Investments' consortium. "The first thing I did was try to find out more information on him," commented Bason. "There have obviously been a large number of foreign owners in English football over the past few decades and fans' experiences of them have varied greatly. So, I guess we were wondering 'what are we getting with Vichai?' Having done some research into Vichai, there were no immediate alarm bells that supporters of other clubs might have had when a takeover happened.

"The one thing Milan Mandaric told us from the outset when he purchased Leicester City in 2007 was that when he did eventually sell the club he would only sell it to someone that could take it further forward. I think that's the biggest thing Mandaric delivered on during his time at Leicester City because King Power have of course been able to take the football club to another level."

In 2011, Vichai succeeded Mandaric as chairman of Leicester City and appointed Top as vice-chair. The club was placed under the direct ownership of King Power International (KPI) – the parent and holding company of the King Power group of companies in September 2012. The following year, King Power Holdings Co Ltd purchased Leicester City's ground – which had become known as the King Power Stadium ahead of the start of the 2011/12 season – for a fee of £17m from previous owners Teachers Insurance. In a statement at that time, the Srivaddhanaprabha family pledged to safeguard the club's long-term future:

"It has always been part of our long-term vision to put the stadium back where it belongs, into the hands of the Football Club. Our plan is to bring long-term sustainable success to Leicester City Football Club. Purchasing the stadium was always a key element in this plan. The previous stadium owners have always been very cooperative. Whilst there are no immediate plans to alter the structure or design of the stadium site, the increased flexibility through direct ownership ensures that the Football Club can freely adjust to the changing needs of its supporter-base for the future."

By this time, King Power seemed to have secured the trust of most of the club's supporters:

"Whenever there's a new chairman or owner at a club, you always tread carefully to begin with in terms of how you view or assess the regime," recalled Bason. "However, by the end of the first year of him being at the club, I think we'd seen enough to start thinking we were in safe hands."

Promotion to the Premier League in 2014 cemented the strength of feeling amongst Foxes' supporters regarding King Power's ownership of the club, The rest, when it came to the story of Vichai and Leicester City, really was history.

King Power expanded their footballing interests in May 2017, with the purchase of Belgian second-tier side Oud-Heverlee Leuven (OHL), who had just finished seventh in the eight-team First Division B table. The club – situated approximately 30km east of Brussels – stated King Power had been the only interested party who made "a clear, written and coherent proposal within the time limit imposed by the board of directors". They added that Vichai's organisation had promised "sufficient financial resources" to aid a promotion push to the Belgian top-flight. The club's home soon became known as the King Power at Den Dreef Stadium.

Early into the 2017/18 season, Dutch manager Dennis van Wijk was replaced by Nigel Pearson – who had previously managed Leicester City under King Power's ownership. Ironically, Top first came across Pearson watching his inaugural football match in England back in 1997, with the former defender playing for Middlesbrough in the League Cup Final that year.

Pearson and King Power enjoyed a successful debut campaign in the Flemish Brabant province, with 'OHL' finishing second in the First Division B table – just three points behind champions Beerschot Wilrijk, who went into the promotion play-offs. Two players were loaned from Leicester City during the season – Elliott Moore and Kamal Sowah – while Thai international Kawin Thamsatchanan arrived from Muangthong United.

The 2018/19 season was far more disappointing, with Leuven ending up in the relegation play-offs. Pearson paid the price for the team's poor form and was sacked on February 3, 2019.

Another of Vichai's major sporting interests was 'King Power Foxes' – a polo team founded in 2014. The high-goal side, which consisted of his sons Tip and Top as well as legendary Argentinian brothers Facundo and Gonzalito Pieres, enjoyed almost overnight success, winning the Gold Cup for three consecutive years between 2015 and 2017. They completed the prestigious British 'double' by also landing the Queen's Cup in 2015. That trophy was presented by Queen Elizabeth II, with Vichai appearing with her in a triumphant team photograph.

The Foxes weren't entered for the 2018 Gold Cup, with King Power choosing to title-sponsor the event at Cowdray Park in West Sussex.

Nicholas Colquhoun-Denvers, president of the Federation of International Polo, explained that Vichai's interest in the sport of polo developed in 1994, when he met Oliver Winter – who is now president of the German Polo Association – at the Bangkok Polo and Equestrian Centre.

"The story goes that Vichai saw this tall German at his club in Bangkok riding a horse and hitting a ball with a stick," said Colquhoun-Denvers. "Vichai asked him what he was doing and Oliver said practicing polo. Vichai proudly said he was a dressage rider to which Oliver responded, 'that's for girls'. Vichai walked away and ignored Oliver for three weeks until one day he came back and asked if he could try polo – the rest is history!

"I met Vichai when he joined our club [Ham Polo Club London or 'HPC'] in the early 2000s. He generously sponsored a few charity matches which he and his sons played in, alongside HRH Prince of Wales and Princes William and Harry on various different occasions. He was always quite shy and retiring but missed nothing and knew exactly what he wanted."

According to Winter, Vichai "learned to play [polo] quite fast" due to his previous experience riding horses.

"I introduced him to polo and the polo community in England in July 1996 where I took him horse riding in Hyde Park one day and to the Cartier International Queen's Cup the next," said Winter. "He was impressed by the set-up and said that he wanted to play there one day too and receive the cup from the Queen!"

Vichai experienced success as a player, winning his first trophy at a tournament at Garden City Polo club in Thailand and competed in the Ladbroke Polo Gold Cup alongside Winter in 1998. He also took part in that competition with long-time friend and fellow future billionaire Harald Link. The King Power owner went on to establish VR Polo Club in Bangkok before being named as president of the Ham Polo Club in 2008 – a role he held for four years. He was honoured by polo's world governing body in 2016 by being named an Ambassador of the Federation of International Polo for his contribution to the development of the sport.

"My father, Mr Vichai Srivaddhanaprabha, was the first Thai polo player [in the Srivaddhanaprabha family]," Top told *The Telegraph* in an interview. "After I had started riding, for four years from age seven to 11 years old, I decided to stop because it felt a bit boring; so football was my new favourite sport. However, my father continued playing polo, built his own field in Pattaya, and took me with him every weekend to watch so I decided to go back on the horse again. We played around the world and my father and I always love to watch the Argentine Open in Palermo, Argentina, so we met many high goal players. We met Marcos Di Paola, he was the first to introduce the Pieres family to us and from that time we planned for the high goal in the UK."

In addition to football and polo, Vichai was a big fan of 'Muay Thai' – a modern integration of several ancient boxing disciplines. Two years after his purchase of Leicester City, Vichai organised 'Thai Fight Extreme' at the King Power Stadium, with event literature describing the sport as follows;

"Muay Thai incorporates the use of hands, feet, knees and elbows. Its popularity in Thailand is already firmly-established, but 'Thai Fight' is aimed at promoting and gaining global recognition for Thai art of self-defence."

In an interview shortly after the event, Vichai explained that he was keen for the club and its supporters to be able to establish an appreciation of Thai culture.

"We would like to give everyone the opportunity to experience it so they can have a greater understanding of Thailand and the values of Thai people," he said. "We would like to share those positive elements of the Kingdom of Thailand. Through football, the people of Leicester have shared an important part of their culture with us and we are determined to give something back.

"Muay Thai is so much more than a sport in Thailand. It is a significant part of our social heritage, so to be able to bring some of the world's elite boxers to King Power Stadium last night was a great privilege. It was our way of celebrating the arrival of the new season and I sincerely hope those in attendance enjoyed the event."

In the latter years of Vichai's life, he became smitten with horse racing. He started to make significant investments at the bloodstock sales towards the end of 2016. By the time of his death in 2018, King Power Racing had 67 horses in training with seven different trainers. The team had 50 winners in its first two years of competition with Beat the Bank, trained by Andrew Balding, winning a series of major races at Ascot and Goodwood in 2018.

Nick Rust, Chief Executive of the British Horseracing Authority, paid tribute to Vichai following his death:

"I didn't personally meet him, but the comments I've heard from those in racing who did suggest that he was a generous and kind man, with a big passion for the sport, who was fair minded and a pleasure to deal with," he commented. "Sometimes when people come in to racing with lots of money, they can be unreasonable, demanding or arrogant, but he was nothing like that.

"He quickly had success at Group Level – the highest echelon of the sport – with Beat the Bank winning Group 2 and Group 3 races. He made a big impact, and his racing organisation has brought some stunning performers to the sport. His colours will be remembered for a long time, and I hope they live on if his family are willing to continue with the operation."

Chapter Four

Foxes on the Hunt

Shortly after suffering the heartbreak of a defeat on penalties to Cardiff City in the Championship Play-Off semi-finals in 2009/10, manager Nigel Pearson departed Leicester City to take the top job at Hull City while Paulo Sousa was installed as his replacement at the Walkers Stadium. A busy summer saw countless players signed and sold, while the biggest arrival of all heading into the 2010/11 campaign was the club's new owners.

When the takeover of the club by Vichai's Asia Football Investments was announced on August 14, 2010 (ratification of the deal was subsequently given by the Football League on October 22, 2010), then-chairman Milan Mandaric stated his belief that the consortium would bring "new strength and energy to Leicester and offer a tremendous opportunity for supporters and the club".

"We are celebrating today" he continued, in a club statement, "as the deal represents three things. First: ambition – this will help us push forward to compete harder for a place at the top table of English football. Second: strength – it will strengthen the squad and Youth Academy by bringing additional financial support and introducing a new global network of contacts and access to player talent.

"It also represents a third key factor: partnership – I am delighted to remain as Chairman and a stakeholder in the new consortia and I am pleased Lee Hoos, the Chief Executive and his winning team remain focussed and in place to keep our plans and ethos alive."

The statement listed Aiyawatt as the head of the consortium taking over the club, but it was ultimately his father Vichai who succeeded Mandaric as Leicester City Chairman on February 10, 2011, while 'Top' became vice-chairman. Outlining the ambition King Power had for the club, Top commented:

"We are delighted that Asia Football Investments has secured this exciting deal; I am passionate about football and I see in Leicester City a club with tremendous passion and potential; it has excellent management on and off the pitch and I am convinced that it has the right mix of ambition and realism to drive the team, and club, forward. I do look forward to getting behind the new manager and his team and to enjoying real progress, which I know the fans crave and deserve."

The 2010/11 season subsequently proved a disappointing one. A run of just one victory in nine Championship matches at the start of the campaign saw new manager Sousa replaced at the Foxes helm by former England boss Sven-Goran Eriksson. The club's form improved, with Leicester just a point off a play-off spot following a 2-1 victory over Bristol City on February 18, 2011. A mixed run of results in the final months saw them end the season in tenth position.

Vichai's influence at Leicester City and his passion for his homeland became instantly apparent, when the team travelled to Thailand in October 2010 for a week-long tour of the country, which included a friendly match against the Thai national team. Martyn Waghorn and Paul Gallagher scored in a 2-0 victory for the Foxes in sweltering conditions at the Suphachalasai Stadium in Bangkok on October 9, 2010.

Trips to the chairman's homeland became commonplace for the Foxes in the years that followed, as a strategic international partnership was forged between the Tourism Authority of Thailand (TAT) and Leicester City. 'Amazing Thailand' branding graced the back of the Foxes shirts for the first two years of the partnership, while that logo was added to the King Power Stadium dugouts too. TAT became a 'Platinum Partner' of the club as well as its official 'Tourism Partner' during Vichai's reign.

Large amounts of money were spent by the club during the 2011/12 season, as attempts were made to try and fulfil Vichai's ambition of Leicester City becoming a Premier League side. The likes of Kasper Schmeichel, Danny Drinkwater and Wes Morgan – all of whom became key members of the Foxes' title-winning side of 2015/16 – were brought to the newly-rebranded 'King Power Stadium' during the campaign. Alas, the Foxes spent most of the season in mid-table, eventually finishing ninth in the Championship.

During the campaign, Nigel Pearson replaced Eriksson as Leicester City manager. Pearson's relationship with the Srivaddhanaprabha family in the years that followed was certainly an intriguing one.

Ahead of Leicester's opening match of the 2012/13 season, Vichai reiterated his ambitions for the club, writing in the Leicester City programme against Peterborough United on August 18, 2012:

"We want to see this club back in the Premier League, the supporters deserve it and we are all determined to do everything we can to get there... We want to achieve long-term, sustainable success, which means investing in areas of the club that will feel the benefit for years to come. The improvements we have made to the stadium, the training ground, the academy and the commercial side are all long-term investments that make us a strong football club financially.

"Success on the pitch is, of course, a little more difficult to control, but in Nigel and his team of staff we have the right people in place to give us the best possible chance of achieving our goals."

Morgan and fellow future title-winner Andy King scored in a 2-0 win over Peterborough that afternoon in front of a home crowd of nearly 24,000. Two consecutive defeats followed in the league but Pearson's men quickly found their stride, claiming top spot in the Championship following a 1-1 draw at Birmingham City on October 20, 2012. A mixed run of results in the months thereafter saw the Foxes drop to fifth position by the end of the year, but they were looking a solid bet to make the play-offs.

Pearson's side achieved just that, with a 3-2 win at Nottingham Forest on the final day of the regular Championship season on May 4, 2013. In the first-leg of their play-off semi-final against Watford, a late goal from David Nugent gave Leicester a one-goal advantage ahead of the second-leg at Vicarage Road three days later. With seconds of stoppage time remaining at the end of that game, the Foxes trailed 2-1 on the day, when they were awarded a penalty.

Anthony Knockaert, who was adjudged to have been fouled by Marco Cassetti in the Hornets box, picked himself up to take the spot kick, with nearly seven minutes of stoppage time having already elapsed. With a place in the Wembley final potentially a kick away for Leicester, the Frenchman's initial effort was saved by goalkeeper Manuel Almunia, who also blocked his follow-up effort. The home side broke quickly and just 20 seconds after Knockaert's penalty was stopped, Troy Deeney fired in an aggregate winner for Watford.

"Do not scratch your eyes, you are really seeing the most extraordinary end to a football match!" screamed Sky Sports commentator Bill Leslie as Leicester City ended up on the wrong side of a moment of cult football history.

The Foxes recovered from the hangover of the previous campaign by triumphing 2-1 at Middlesbrough on the opening day of the 2013/14 season. Jamie Vardy, who had been recruited from Fleetwood Town a year earlier, got the match winner at the Riverside Stadium.

The season would see Leicester City set all kinds of club records, as they won the Championship title in style, amassing 102 points. The class of 2013/14 achieved the Foxes' most league wins in a single campaign (31) and their longest consecutive run of league matches in which they scored (32). They also managed their largest number of home league victories (17) and their joint-best run of away league triumphs (14).

After their emphatic promotion to the Premier League, Vichai organised a post-season trip to Bangkok, during which he and the players were pictured with the Championship trophy. During a press conference, the King Power boss outlined his future ambitions for his now, top-flight, football club.

"We should be able to stay [in the Premier League] for at least two or three years and then my next goal will be taking the team to the top five or six in the Premier League," he told reporters.

"It will take a huge amount of money, possibly 10bn [£180m], to get there. That doesn't put us off. I am asking for three years, and we'll be there [in the Premier League's top five]. We won't take the huge leap to challenge the league's top five clubs immediately. Do we have a chance to beat them? Yes, we have, but I think we need to establish our foothold in the league first and then we think about our next step."

Vichai's ambitions of establishing the Foxes as a top-five Premier League outfit within three years and his pledge to invest some £180m in the team certainly raised some eyebrows back in Leicester.

"We [Leicester City supporters] laughed at that suggestion, thinking 'you're getting a bit carried away now!" remembered Foxes Trust chairman Ian Bason, on hearing Vichai's comments in May 2014. "The ambition for the majority of fans going into that first season back in the Premier League was stay up… it was as simple as that. If we stayed in the division, the ambition was to stay there another season and eventually become a solid Premier League side that never really got dragged into the relegation dog-fight. The thought of being a club challenging for a top six or seven place seemed pretty far off to be honest."

Leicester made a second trip to Thailand in the summer of 2014, to play an exhibition match against Premier League rivals Everton at the Supachalasai Stadium in Bangkok on July 27 that year. The previous day, the squad had attended the opening of a Leicester City fan store at BTS Siam station in the city, with the new shop emphasising the growth in popularity of the so-called 'Siamese Foxes' in Vichai's homeland.

Leicester drew 2-2 with Everton in Vichai's first match as chairman of a Premier League club on August 16, 2014, while they also managed a credible draw with Arsenal and a 1-0 victory at Stoke City in the opening months of the campaign. Then, an incredible 5-3 victory over Manchester United at the King Power Stadium on September 21, 2014 saw the Foxes rise to seventh in the league.

Any thoughts of Leicester mounting an ahead-of-schedule push for the Premier League's top five were quickly dashed though, with a run of 13 matches without a win in the division. Indeed, the Foxes only picked up two points in between a 2-0 defeat at Crystal Palace on September 27, 2014 and a 2-1 home loss to Tottenham Hotspur on Boxing Day 2014. The two wins and a draw that followed the game against Spurs felt somewhat in vain as the Foxes remained rooted to the bottom of the table.

"It [2014/15] was a strange season because for the majority of it, we had played well but time and time again, we didn't pick up the result... we'd often lose by the odd goal," commented Bason. "Despite playing well, it did get to the point in the campaign when relegation started to feel inevitable. I went on local radio on a fans' forum after a defeat to Manchester City [on March 4, 2015]. All three studio guests, myself included said 'if we don't win the next game, we're going to get relegated'. We went and drew 0-0 with Hull City at home [on March 14, 2015] in that next game and there was definitely a feeling of 'that's it, we've had it now' after that result."

A run of eight matches without a win between January 17 and March 21, 2015 left Leicester on the brink of relegation – some seven points from safety, albeit with a game in hand on a number of teams in the bottom six. According to *MailOnline*, there came a day in February 2015 when Vichai decided to sack Nigel Pearson, only for Top to convince his father to "reverse the decision".

If that story is true, Top's intervention was an inspired one. Four straight victories over West Ham United, West Bromwich Albion, Swansea City and Burnley saw Leicester climb out of the Premier League's bottom three with five matches of the campaign remaining.

"It is still unclear what sparked that revival," commented Bason. "There were rumours that [then Foxes midfielder] Esteban Cambiasso called the team together at one stage and said 'we're going to do this and that' going forward. But when you read [Jamie] Vardy's book [*From Nowhere*], it didn't seem he particularly got on with Cambiasso... and possibly that was the case for some of the other players... so the catalyst for the turnaround is definitely unclear.

"On the pitch, the 2-1 win over West Ham seemed like the turning point in the season. Whenever you get a victory late on in a match, it always seems to give players and supporters a particular lift and belief going forward."

After a 3-1 home defeat to Chelsea on April 30, 2015, Leicester's unlikely Premier League survival was confirmed with victories over Newcastle United, Southampton and Queens Park Rangers at the King Power Stadium and a goalless draw at Sunderland. It was during that period that news of some kind gifts given to Foxes supporters by Vichai hit the headlines. He followed up the offer of a free breakfast for the 3,000 or so fans that went to Sunderland on May 16,

HRH Prince Charles and president of the Thailand Polo Association Vichai Raksriaksorn at the Chakravarty Cup Polo match between Team Thailand and Team Dubai played at the Ham Polo Club on **June 11, 2005** in Richmond, England.

Leicester City's owner Vichai Raksriaksorn in the stands, **October 26, 2010.**

Images of Leicester City players Jamie Vardy, Shinji Okazaki and Kasper Schmeichel in front of the King Power Downtown Complex, Bangkok, Thailand, **April 24, 2016.**

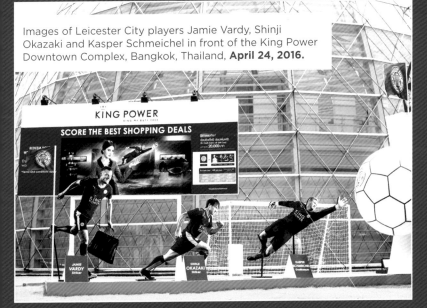

Leicester City's Jamie Vardy celebrates scoring his side's third goal of the game from the penalty spot in front of Everton goalkeeper Joel Robles during the Barclays Premier League match at the King Power Stadium, Leicester, **May 7, 2016.**

Leicester City players celebrate winning the Barclays Premier League, after the match at the King Power Stadium, Leicester, **May 7, 2016.**

Leicester City's team on the bus as fans look on during the open top bus parade through Leicester City Centre, **May 16, 2016.**

Leicester City fans celebrate alongside the team, on stage, in Victoria Park after the open top bus parade through Leicester City Centre, **May 16, 2016.**

Vichai Srivaddhanaprabha, Club President of Leicester City Football Club, during press release and interview at Aksra Theatre of King Power Downtown Complex, Rangnam, Bangkok, Thailand, **May 18, 2016.**

The Leicester City team parade the Premier League trophy as thousands of fans turn out to the open-top bus celebration in Bangkok, Thailand, **May 19, 2016.**

Leicester City arrive in Bangkok to a hero's welcome on Sukhumvit Road, Bangkok, Thailand, **May 19, 2016.**

Leicester City Chairman Vichai Srivaddhanaprabha acknowledges the fans after the Premier League match at the King Power Stadium, Leicester, **May 21, 2017.**

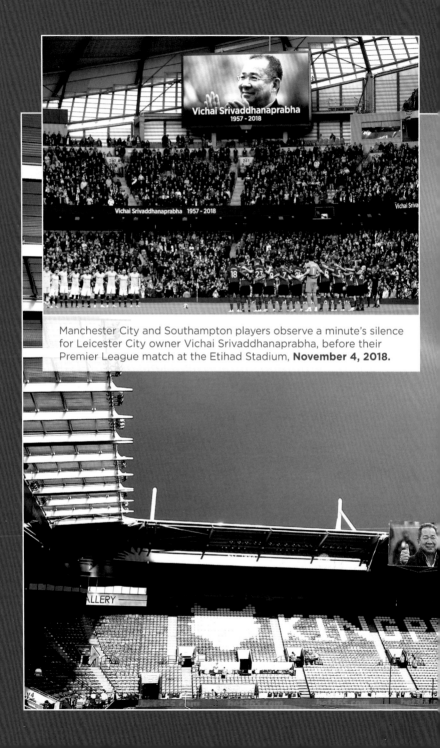

Manchester City and Southampton players observe a minute's silence for Leicester City owner Vichai Srivaddhanaprabha, before their Premier League match at the Etihad Stadium, **November 4, 2018.**

Leicester City players arrive at Wat Thepsirin for the funeral of Vichai Srivaddhanaprabha in Bangkok, Thailand, **November 4, 2018.**

EVER IN
HEARTS

A rainbow emerges over the King Power Stadium before the match where a big screen displays a tribute image to Vichai Srivaddhanaprabha which reads 'Forever in our hearts', **November 10, 2018.**

Fans view floral tributes for those who lost their lives in the helicopter crash, **November 10, 2018.**

Fans hold scarves for Leicester City Chairman Vichai Srivaddhanaprabha during the Premier League match at the King Power Stadium, Leicester, **November 10, 2018.**

2015 with a free beer – or a bottle of water – for every person that went to the home game against Queens Park Rangers the following week:

"We want to say thank you to our fans for their incredible support this season," he said. "It's been key in the team securing another season in the top flight."

During that same season, the BBC Sport's *Price of Football* study found that the Foxes offered the cheapest day out in the Premier League, with a ticket, pie, programme and a cup of tea costing as little as £27.50.

After completing their Premier League 'great escape' act, Leicester City travelled to Thailand for another post-season goodwill tour. On the club's return, the Foxes dismissed three academy players – manager Nigel Pearson's son James as well as teammates Tom Hopper and Adam Smith – for their inappropriate behaviour whilst in Bangkok.

Just 13 days after James Pearson left the King Power Stadium, the Foxes terminated his father's contract citing "fundamental differences in perspective" between the board of directors and the departing manager.

"The board of directors recognises the success Nigel has helped to bring to Leicester City during his two spells in charge of the club, particularly during the last three and a half years," read a club statement.

"Regrettably, the club believes that the working relationship between Nigel and the board is no longer viable. We trust that the club's supporters will recognise that the owners have always acted with the best interests of the club at heart and with the club's long-term future as their greatest priority."

Nigel Pearson went on to work for another King Power-owned club – OH Leuven – for whom he was manager between September 22, 2017 and February 3, 2019.

Bookmaker Betfair installed former Foxes midfielder Neil Lennon as an early favourite to replace Pearson at the King Power Stadium offering odds of 3-1. Sam Allardyce, Sean Dyche, Roberto Di Matteo, Steve Cotterill and Martin O'Neill's names were also mentioned in dispatches. The club's veteran midfielder Esteban Cambiasso was even seen as a 12-1 shot by bet365.

Pearson's ultimate replacement largely managed to fly under the radar, prior to his appointment on July 13, 2015. His identity was to be the first of a series of major surprises Vichai and Leicester City were about to pull off over the coming 12 months.

Chapter Five

The Impossible Dream

Gary Lineker was clearly unimpressed by the appointment of Claudio Ranieri as the manager of his former club Leicester City in July 2015. "Claudio Ranieri? Really?" tweeted the BBC *Match of the Day* presenter, who later described the Italian as an "uninspired choice by Leicester." Former Tottenham Hotspur boss Harry Redknapp also took to social media to suggest Ranieri had "done well to get the Leicester job" after being sacked after just four matches in charge of the Greece national team prior to that. Another ex-Leicester player, Tony Cottee, simply commented that he was "astonished" by the appointment.

Foxes supporters had a somewhat lukewarm reaction to the news of Ranieri's arrival at the King Power Stadium too.

"There were some supporters that wondered if he were a bit old hat and past his best," said Foxes Trust Chairman Ian Bason. "Others looked at the success he had in his career and thought he might well be able to have an impact at Leicester.

"Whenever there's a managerial change, from a personal perspective it's usually a case of, 'ask me my thoughts in a year's time'. You can look at past reputation but you can never know if the manager and the players or the club culture will fit. We've had managers at the club we thought would do well and didn't and vice-versa."

Amidst all the opinion, there was one man never in doubt about Ranieri's appointment. Vichai's son Top interviewed the Italian for the job that summer and soon recommended him to his father for a second, final interview.

"At that time there were a number of managers I got in to interview," Top told *MailOnline*. "Claudio was my first choice – even though I had three or four more to interview. He had something special on that day and when he spoke he said everything I wanted to hear. All the plans I had in my head, he said them out loud. The way he wanted to manage the team was the right way for what the club wanted."

While there was confidence in Ranieri within the King Power Stadium – Top even declaring him as "one of the world's elite managers" at a press confidence – the bookmakers were not impressed, with a number cutting Leicester's odds of getting relegated in 2015/16 from 7-2 to 11-4. Two of the country's leading firms, Ladbrokes and William Hill, were offering odds of 5,000-1 on the Foxes winning the title meanwhile.

The season began well for Leicester, who topped the Premier League table after the first two rounds of fixtures with victories over Sunderland and West Ham United. They then drew 1-1 with Tottenham Hotspur on August 22, 2015.

The momentum of the previous 'great escape' season continued, as the Foxes extended their unbeaten start to the campaign to six matches with draws with AFC Bournemouth and Stoke City and an impressive victory over Aston Villa on September 13, 2015 that saw Ranieri's team come back from two goals down to win 3-2.

"Ranieri just seemed to do everything right in his first season" commented Bason. "I remember that match when we came from behind to beat Aston Villa. His substitutions that day worked a treat and they seemed to work throughout the season. I particularly remember in the first half of the campaign... he'd always bring someone on who went on to make the difference."

Leicester's first defeat of the season came at the hands of Arsenal – who had been unbeaten themselves at the start of the 2015/16 campaign. Despite a brace from Jamie Vardy, the Gunners ran out 5-2 winners at the King Power Stadium.

Ranieri was phlegmatic after the defeat and told the media: "We are sad because we wanted to continue to be unbeaten. But when you play against Arsenal, United, Chelsea, City, it's extra. It is important to learn something. What is very important is the reaction in the next match. We are down. But our spirit must be very high."

Despite Leicester being only four points behind table-toppers Manchester City after that defeat, odds of 5,000-1 were still available at that stage of the campaign on the Foxes becoming Premier League champions. Over the coming months though, Ranieri's men showed themselves to be more than mere early season pace-setters. A run of eight wins and two draws in their next ten matches saw the Foxes take a five-point lead at the top of the table after their 3-2 victory at Everton on December 19, 2015.

In Leicester's 1-1 draw with Manchester United on November 28, 2015, Jamie Vardy broke ex-Red Devils striker Ruud van Nistelrooy's record, as he became the first player to score in 11 consecutive Premier League matches. Algerian winger Riyad Mahrez, signed from Le Havre back in 2014, was emerging as another star of the season for the Foxes. His brace of penalties in the aforementioned victory at Goodison Park took his league goal tally for the campaign to 13.

A defeat to Liverpool on Boxing Day 2015, coupled with back-to-back goalless draws with Manchester City and AFC

Bournemouth, saw the Foxes briefly relinquish the top spot. A 1-0 victory at Tottenham Hotspur on January 13, 2016 – who proved to be Leicester's main title rivals for the majority of the season – was a pivotal result, as was a 1-1 draw at Aston Villa three days later, which returned the club to the summit.

On January 22, 2016, Vichai received an honorary degree of Doctor of Laws from the University of Leicester. In a brief acceptance speech at De Montfort Hall, he commented:

"It is my great honour to stand on this honourable step today. I am so proud to be part of Leicester City and today, I am more proud to be part of the University of Leicester. I promise to do my best for our Leicester, for the university and the football club."

He expanded on his speech after the ceremony, expressing his love for Leicester City Football Club:

"I would like to express my thanks to the University of Leicester for this great honour and to the people of Leicester for the warm welcome they have extended to me, my family and colleagues since King Power first arrived in the city.

"I feel very fortunate because I do what I love, so I put love into everything I do. I came to the football industry with Leicester City because of my love for football and the club and its fans have already repaid me several times over with their passion and loyalty. It is a great privilege to be the Chairman of this great club and an accepted member of this wonderful community.

"What has impressed me the most is the people of Leicester and their united will for us to succeed. My family and I cannot achieve our ambitions for the club alone, so an honour such as this is as much for the people of Leicester as it is for me."

Wins for Vichai's beloved Leicester City over Stoke City and Liverpool at the King Power Stadium were perfect preparation for a crunch encounter at another of the club's title rivals – Manchester City – on February 6, 2016. Robert Huth, who had scored the winner at White Hart Lane a month earlier, put the Foxes one-up in that game, while Mahrez doubled their lead shortly after half-time. Huth's second goal of the day on the hour mark put the game beyond the Cityzens, who got a late consolation through Sergio Aguero.

"There was the comment throughout the season of 'they're [Leicester] going to fall away'," commented Bason. "The hopes that we could win the title intensified as the season went on, but of course there was always that doubt. The seminal result for me was the victory at Manchester City. That was the moment I thought, 'ok, we really could be champions'. But you never say aloud that you think you're going to be champions until it actually happens."

A 2-1 defeat for Leicester at Arsenal on Valentine's Day cut the Foxes' lead at the top to two points and saw the Gunners installed as 13-8 favourites for the title. Spurs – who won 2-1 at Manchester City that same weekend – were now 5-2 second favourites. Both north London clubs would struggle in the weeks that followed with Arsenal losing 3-2 at Manchester United on February 28 while Tottenham were beaten 1-0 at West Ham United on March 2 – a night after Leicester had been held to a 2-2 draw at home by West Bromwich Albion.

A run of five consecutive victories in March and early April saw Leicester City close in on the Premier League trophy.

Manchester City's goalless draw at Norwich City on March 12 saw the Foxes installed as odds-on favourites to win the title at 10-11. On April 3, Vichai celebrated his upcoming birthday by offering Foxes supporters a free Singha Beer and Krispy Kreme doughnuts ahead of the 1-0 victory over Southampton.

While a 2-2 draw with West Ham United and a sending-off for Jamie Vardy in that match on April 17 was a slight set-back, the side bounced back with an emphatic 4-0 victory over Swansea City the following week. While Vichai and wife Aimon could be seen celebrating that win in the Directors' Box at the King Power Stadium, son Top was watching on a big screen at the company's headquarters around 6,000 miles away in Bangkok. "We have 600 people come to celebrate and enjoy to watch Leicester, the team that maybe seven years ago no one knew," Top told journalists at the match screening.

Tottenham's 1-1 draw at home to West Bromwich Albion that following day left Leicester requiring just three more points to be champions. The Foxes were unable to seal the title in their next game, as they drew 1-1 at Manchester United. However, Ranieri's men would only have to wait just a little over 24 hours to complete their most unlikely fairy tale.

Tottenham Hotspur travelled to Stamford Bridge to face Chelsea on May 2, knowing they needed a win to keep the title race alive. They took a 2-0 half-time lead with goals from ex-Leicester loanee Harry Kane and South Korean international Son Heung-Min. The Blues struck back in the second-half through Gary Cahill before Eden Hazard levelled seven minutes from time. The final whistle was the cue for scenes of raucous celebrations in the East Midlands.

Pictures of Leicester City players in raptures, partying at Jamie Vardy's house, soon emerged on social media and on Sky Sports' live broadcast of the Chelsea-Spurs match. Supporters lined the streets of the city while Gary Lineker marked the momentous occasion by opening a bottle of champagne, telling the BBC; "never, ever, ever, ever, in my lifetime did I believe it was even remotely possible that Leicester would win any kind of league, let alone the Premier League. Get in!"

Vichai's whereabouts on this night of nights for Leicester City isn't known, but Top spoke on Thai television to reflect his father's view that winning the Premier League "was not what we dared to dream" when the Asian Football Investments consortium purchased the club in 2010.

"He [Vichai] was already proud of being the owner of an English Premier League team. Now he has owned an English Premier League champion team, he can't be prouder. I have to say on his behalf that he has managed the club with his heart and he just hopes to gain a reputation for the country [of Thailand]."

Leicester City hosted Everton in their penultimate match of the Premier League season, with the trophy presentation arranged for after the game. Vichai penned his own thoughts in that afternoon's matchday programme.

"I always believed in the power of our spirit," he wrote. "It drove us to reach the Premier League, it gave us the strength to stay in the Premier League, and now it has inspired us to win the Premier League. It is a spirit that has spread beyond Leicester, taking our story to the hearts of the world. Our spirit exists because of the love we share for each other and the energy it helps to create, both on and off the pitch, and in the years to come, it will continue to be our greatest asset."

The Foxes extended their unbeaten run to 11 fixtures that afternoon, racing into a two-goal lead before half-time through strikes from Vardy and Andy King. A Vardy penalty made it three on 65 minutes before Kevin Mirallas grabbed a late consolation for the visitors. Pre-match, supporters at the King Power Stadium were given a real treat as Italian opera singer Andrea Bocelli performed *Nessun Dorma* and *Con Te Partiro*, while a clearly emotional Claudio Ranieri stood alongside him.

After the 3-1 win, the Srivaddhanaprabha family headed down onto the pitch for the trophy presentation, receiving a standing ovation as they did so. The stadium announcer heralded Vichai and Top's entrance and thanked them for "turning the fortunes of the club on its head" before welcoming club legend Alan 'The Birch' Birchenall MBE onto the field, carrying the Premier League trophy.

"It was a really nice touch from the owners that they got Birch to take the trophy out onto the pitch," commented Bason. "He's obviously been at the club for years and it would have meant so much to him."

Birchenall told the *Leicester Mercury* he would be "forever indebted" to Vichai for that "unbelievable moment", adding, "It is not overstating to say that without Vichai that would not have happened. The club would not have lifted the title. He made the impossible possible. He allowed us to dream and we did, then woke up and it was real – we had won the league."

Vichai and Top stood at the head of a line of club staff that embraced the players as they walked towards a podium that had been assembled in the centre of the King Power Stadium pitch. Foxes supporter Steve Worthy then had the dream job of handing over the Premier League trophy to club captain Wes Morgan, who held it aloft.

Vichai and Top joined in with a team photograph, with the chairman proudly gripping the trophy while his son sat with Peter Schmeichel and PFA Player of the Year, Riyad Mahrez. After the presentation, Top briefly addressed the supporters. "Hello champions," he said to a cheering crowd. "I think we need a bigger stadium, huh?"

Leicester City had hit the big time. In the days after the title success, New York-based research firm Private Company Financial Intelligence valued the club at £436m – 11 times what Vichai paid for the Foxes back in 2010. Agent and sports lawyer David Seligman meanwhile valued the club's Premier League-winning team "upwards of £200m". The squad had been assembled for £57m, with Jamie Vardy having signed for the club for just £1m in 2012, while Mahrez was a £400,000 capture in 2014.

"If you take Jamie Vardy and Riyad Mahrez as individuals, you're looking at £70m there," said Seligman, who also discussed the meteoric rise in value of N'Golo Kante with the BBC. The French midfielder arrived at the King Power Stadium from Caen for £5.6m prior to the start of the campaign.

Not that Vichai had any thoughts on selling either the club or his star players. Just a few days after sealing their Premier League title success, Top told the BBC's Dan Roan that the club were already scouting new talent for the following season.

"We will build the team to compete in the Premier League," he said. "We will compete in the Champions League next season and I am not saying we will win the big cup, but we will try. We want to keep our best players and we will add some quality players with the right people. I am not sure where we will finish next season.

"We will try to win the league again. The target is the same, we want to build the squad and we try to stay in the Premier League as long as we can. To win the title again is so difficult. It will be super difficult from now. If we win, we win."

It seemed fitting, given Vichai's promise – outlined by Top in the book, *The Fairy Tale of Underfox* – "to buy a football team that can compete with Chelsea" that the Foxes' final match of the season should take place at Stamford Bridge. The Blues – who had played their own part in Leicester's success by securing the draw with Spurs that sealed the Foxes' title – gave the visitors a champions' guard of honour as they walked out onto the pitch for the match. Claudio Ranieri's former employers also presented the manager with an engraved silver plate. The game, played close to Vichai's London home, finished in a 1-1 draw, with Danny Drinkwater getting a late equaliser for Leicester that afternoon.

The following day, the players and staff went on an open-bus parade around the city of Leicester, with an estimated 240,000 people greeting them on their journey from Jubilee Square to Victoria Park. Vichai and family took to the park stage for another lifting of the trophy. Rock band Kasabian – whose members are originally from Leicester and huge Foxes fans – opened their set at the event by declaring "this one is for the underdogs".

Celebrations continued in Thailand a few days later as Leicester City touched down in Bangkok on May 18, 2016. Another trophy parade took place, with an open top bus carrying players and staff as well as Vichai and Top around the Thai capital, led by a convoy of Thai tuk-tuks adorned with the club's crest. An estimated one million well-wishers turned out to see the so-called 'Siamese Foxes', with the celebratory trip starting and ending at King Power's headquarters on Rangnam Road. The team also visited the Grand Palace – home to King Bhumipol Adulyadej, who died later that year – as well as the Wat Traimit temple in the Chinatown district, where Vichai was a long-time devotee and benefactor, during their stay.

Amongst those on the crowded streets of Bangkok during the Foxes' visit was Leicester City supporter Chatworachet Sae-Kow, who expressed his pride in the team's success under Vichai's ownership to the world's media. "It's Thailand's team," said Chatworachet. "It brought fame to Thailand when they won [the title]. He [Vichai] carried the Thai flag with him and made people know more about Thailand."

There was praise for Vichai back in Leicester too. Ian Bason, Chairman of the Foxes Trust told *The Guardian*: "It would be hard to criticise him [Vichai] at all.

"Other than what the club has actually achieved, [the owners] have always listened to the fans," continued Bason. "Vichai has always respected the heritage of the club."

Chapter Six

Dining at the Top Table

Leicester City warmed up for their title-winning campaign in 2015/16 by facing the likes of Lincoln City, Mansfield Town, Burton Albion and Rotherham United in pre-season friendlies. Twelve months on – and as reigning champions of England – their preparations for the defence of their Premier League crown were somewhat different.

As well as taking on Manchester United at Wembley Stadium in the FA Community Shield – the traditional curtain-raiser to the domestic season – the Foxes competed in the International Champions Cup. They played some of the game's big-hitters in that pre-season tournament in the shape of Celtic, Paris Saint-Germain and Barcelona. The clashes with those European heavyweights were a taste of things to come for the club, who took their place in the UEFA Champions League group stage draw in Monaco on August 25, 2016.

It's fair to say Leicester's continental experience prior to that date was minimal. The Foxes had never previously progressed beyond the first round stage of a European competition, having briefly taken part in the European Cup Winners' Cup in 1961/62 and the UEFA Cup in 1997/98 and 2000/01. While few were expecting Ranieri's men to challenge the likes of Real Madrid, Barcelona, Bayern Munich and Juventus for the trophy, odds of 100-1 on Leicester winning the Champions League showed that the bookmakers considered the possibility of the club pulling off another miracle to be vaguely plausible.

The bookies had learnt not to underestimate Leicester the hard way. In May 2016, Betfair paid out £200,000 to one punter who had put a £100 bet on the club winning the Premier League back in October 2015, while another cashed-out on a £50 pre-season bet on the Foxes a few months before the season end, collecting £72,335 from Ladbrokes. William Hill, the UK's biggest bookmaker, processed their largest-ever pay out on the Premier League – £3m, representing a £2.2m loss – on the back of the club's success.

When you consider that Sporting Lisbon were in a group with Borussia Dortmund and Real Madrid, PSV Eindhoven were paired with the likes of Bayern and Atletico Madrid and Celtic took their place alongside Barcelona and Manchester City, the Champions League group stage draw appeared to have been relatively kind to Leicester. Ranieri's side, aided by being one of the draw's eight top seeds, took their place in Group G along with Porto, Copenhagen and Club Brugge.

Before their European campaign got underway with a trip to Brugge on September 14, 2016, the Foxes kicked off their Premier League season with a disappointing 2-1 loss at newly-promoted Hull City. Leicester's home form in the opening months was good, with victories over Swansea City, Burnley and Crystal Palace and draws with Arsenal and Southampton. But on the road, they suffered heavy defeats to Liverpool, Manchester United and Chelsea, leaving them in tenth position in the league by the end of October.

Leicester's European adventures proved a welcome distraction from their indifferent domestic form. A brace from Riyad Mahrez helped the Foxes to a 3-0 away win at Club Brugge on their Champions League debut, while they followed that up with back-to-back 1-0 home wins over Porto and Copenhagen.

A goalless draw in Copenhagen on November 2, 2016 left Ranieri's team requiring just a point from one of their two remaining group stage fixtures to make the knockout phase of the competition. Their passage to the last 16 was sealed with a 2-1 triumph over Club Brugge at the King Power Stadium on November 22, 2016 – a result which meant their heavy 5-0 defeat in Porto a few weeks later could largely be consigned to history.

The club's Premier League form was far more concerning. A 2-2 draw at home to Middlesbrough on November 26, 2016 left Leicester just two points above the relegation zone. Ranieri realised the growing seriousness of the Foxes' situation and commented in his post-match press conference: "They [Leicester's players] have to play with pressure. They must remember not how last season went but two seasons ago, they now must be focused on this. We have to play with the same character as the season then – the 'great escape'".

A 2-1 away defeat at bottom side Sunderland a week later compounded Leicester's poor run of results – their return of 13 points after 14 games was the worst return of any defending champion in Premier League history. The loss came just a day after it had been announced that Ranieri was one of the three finalists nominated for the 2015 Best FIFA Men's Coach – an award he subsequently won early in the new year.

The under-fire manager was asked about his future in a press conference ahead of Leicester's final Champions League group game, to which he responded; "Am I worried about the sack? Never, because it's not my decision. The owner is always behind us, of course he's not happy, no one at the club is.

When we win, we win together, when we lose, we lose together. My experience says it's important to stay calm and be positive, believe in your players and do the best for your team."

Football was very much put into perspective on January 12, 2017, when Leicester City ambassador Alan 'The Birch' Birchenall collapsed shortly after presenting an award at the *Leicester Mercury* Sports Awards. Over 500 guests were left in stunned silence as the legendary former player was treated with a defibrillator. It was later revealed he had 'died' for seven minutes having suffered a cardiac arrest. Fortunately, the ex-midfielder – who made 163 appearances for the Foxes, scoring 12 goals – made a good recovery. He returned to the King Power Stadium for the first time after his heart attack for a match against Stoke City in March, in which he was guest of the Srivaddhanaprabha family in the club's Directors Box.

Deloitte published their annual *Football Money League* report in January 2017, which revealed the world's richest football clubs by turnover during the 2015/16 season. The incredible job done by Vichai and King Power since taking over at the East Midlands side in 2010 – not to mention the miracle of the club winning the Premier League – was emphasised by Leicester's City's first-ever appearance in the top 20 listings. The Foxes' revenue rose 23% to £128.7m from £104.4m the previous year.

While the club's finances looked rosy, Leicester's inconsistency on the pitch continued in the opening months of 2017, as speculation started to mount over Ranieri's future at the King Power Stadium. True to his usual form, Vichai was tight-lipped – publicly at least – regarding the situation. It wasn't until

February 7, 2017 – while the Foxes remained without a win that calendar year – that comment finally came from the higher echelons of the club, in the form of a statement backing their much-maligned manager.

"The entire club is and will remain united behind its manager," read the statement. "The unprecedented success achieved in recent seasons has been based firmly on stability, togetherness and determination to overcome the greatest of challenges."

A run of five Premier League defeats, an FA Cup exit at the hands of Millwall and a 2-1 loss to Sevilla in the first leg of the Foxes' Champions League round of 16 tie signalled a swift re-think from Vichai and co. On February 23, 2017 – a day after that match in Spain – it was announced Ranieri's contract at the club had been terminated.

Top told the media: "This has been the most difficult decision we have had to make in nearly seven years since King Power took ownership of Leicester City. But we are duty-bound to put the Club's long-term interests above all sense of personal sentiment, no matter how strong that might be.

"Claudio has brought outstanding qualities to his office. His skilful management, powers of motivation and measured approach have been reflective of the rich experience we always knew he would bring to Leicester City. His warmth, charm and charisma have helped transform perceptions of the Club and develop its profile on a global scale. We will forever be grateful to him for what he has helped us to achieve.

"It was never our expectation that the extraordinary feats of last season should be replicated this season. Indeed, survival in the Premier League was our first and only target at the start of the campaign. But we are now faced with a fight to reach that objective and feel a change is necessary to maximise the opportunity presented by the final 13 games."

Assistant Manager Craig Shakespeare and First Team Coach Mike Stowell were put in temporary charge of the team ahead of the Foxes match at home to Liverpool. As the football world had been shocked by Ranieri's appointment at Leicester in the first place, there was a high level of surprise – despite the club's poor form – that the hierarchy would dismiss a manager who had won them the Premier League title less than a year earlier.

Gary Lineker, who had once derided Leicester City's decision to give Ranieri the top job at the King Power Stadium, said the Italian's departure had left him "inexplicable, unforgivable and gut-wrenchingly sad".

"What happened last season was pretty extraordinary under Claudio Ranieri and I think the lack of gratitude from the owners of the club – and who knows who else is involved in such a decision – beggars belief," added Lineker in an interview with BBC Radio 4's *Today* programme.

Ian Bason, Chairman of the Foxes Trust, shared in Lineker's disappointment with Ranieri's exit from the King Power Stadium:

"It felt too early to me," said Bason. "There were very mixed feelings about it from fans. You could see it wasn't quite working on the pitch. He was trying to change things and it wasn't quite panning out. But at the time, it felt a bit harsh and I think most fans felt he could have been given longer. One of the hardest factors in seeing him go was knowing what Ranieri is like as a person, how he behaved around the media, the supporters etc. There was a definite sadness about his departure."

There was early vindication for the club's decision to axe Ranieri as the Foxes beat Liverpool 3-1 in Craig Shakespeare's first match in charge of the side on February 27, 2017. Leicester's turnaround continued with a 3-1 win over Hull City, prompting King Power's decision to confirm Shakespeare's appointment until the end of the season on March 12, 2017. Two days later, the rookie boss helped orchestrate one of the finest results in the club's history as goals from Wes Morgan and Marc Albrighton saw them to a 2-0 victory over Sevilla, to secure progress to the quarter final stage of the Champions League with a 3-2 aggregate success.

Wins over West Ham United and Stoke City in the Premier League continued Shakespeare's 100% record at the start of his Leicester managerial career as Vichai prepared to celebrate his 59th birthday. As had become customary, the chairman provided gifts to supporters at the closest home game to his anniversary, with beer and cupcakes handed out prior to the match against Sunderland on April 4, 2017. The team presented Vichai with their own present – a 2-0 victory over the Black Cats thanks to goals from Islam Slimani and Jamie Vardy.

Shakespeare experienced his first defeat as Leicester City manager on April 9, 2017 as the Foxes went down to a 4-2 away loss at Everton. Three days later, they were beaten 1-0 by Atletico Madrid at the Vicente Calderón stadium in the first leg of their Champions League quarter final tie. A 1-1 draw with the Spanish side at the King Power Stadium a week later saw Shakespeare's men make an honourable exit from Europe's premier club competition. 'Los Colchoneros' had now been responsible for eliminating Leicester for a third time from a European tournament in only their fourth continental campaign.

Leicester experienced a mixed run of results as the season drew towards an end – including a 6-1 home thrashing by Tottenham Hotspur on May 18, 2017. By this point in the campaign, the Foxes had long since ensured their Premier League survival, finishing 12th in the division a year on from winning it. Shakespeare's reward for steadying the ship at the King Power Stadium was a three-year managerial contract, which he duly signed on June 8, 2017.

Alas, one win in eight Premier League matches at the start of the 2017/18 season saw that contract terminated after the Foxes had fallen into the bottom three. Claude Puel, who had guided Southampton to the League Cup Final and an eighth-place finish in the league the previous campaign, replaced Shakespeare. The incoming Frenchman was heralded by Top in a club statement:

"When we began the process of identifying a new manager, the Board quickly established the profile of the candidate we needed to take the club forward and Claude Puel was a perfect fit," said the vice-chairman.

Puel's first match in charge of the Foxes saw them beat Everton 2-0 in the Premier League on October 19, 2017, while Leicester managed runs to the quarter finals in both domestic cup competitions in his debut season at the King Power Stadium. Leicester once again featured in the *Deloitte Football Money League*, published in January 2018. The Foxes rose six places in the listings to become the 14th wealthiest club in the world, based on turnover revenue during the 2016/17 season, that saw them compete in the Champions League for the first time.

The Foxes turnover in 2016/17 increased from £128.7m in the previous campaign to £233m. They were one of a record ten clubs from the Premier League to feature in the top 20, with those English teams generating a total revenue of 3.8bn between them in the first year of a new broadcasting deal. Around the same time, it was revealed that Vichai's personal wealth had risen an estimated $0.5bn over the past 12 months, putting him fifth on Forbes' list of Thailand's richest people. The publication stated his net worth at $5.2bn (£3.8bn), up from $4.7bn the previous year.

Celebrations to mark Vichai's birthday in 2018 were particularly special, as the chairman turned 60. Aside from the customary free beer for supporters, 60 fans had their season ticket for the 2018/19 campaign renewed by the chairman free of charge while there was an impressive fireworks display prior to the 2-1 home defeat to Newcastle United on April 7, 2018. Chocolate coins, carrying the club crest and the message 'Happy Birthday Mr Chairman' were also distributed that afternoon.

From January 31, 2018 through to the end of the campaign, the Foxes recorded just three league victories. Having taken Leicester City from 18th position when he joined to ninth place by the season's conclusion, Puel's overall impact could be judged as a positive one. By the closing weeks of the campaign though, there was a clear mood of dissatisfaction amongst supporters regarding the team's performance and the manager's tactics.

"At first it seemed that Puel's change of style and approach had been seamlessly embraced by the players," surmised the

Leicester Mercury's Rob Tanner after the 2-0 home defeat to West Ham United on May 5, 2018. "He immediately switched to a new formation and City did play entertaining attacking football. However, recently, it is hard to spot what the game plan is as the players appear lacking in inspiration or direction."

A number of days before that game against West Ham, Vichai had flown in from Thailand, with Tanner speculating his presence was to both "show his support, but also to deliver a subtle kick up the bum". For once, the chairman's presence didn't appear to have the desired effect and after the final whistle sounded following the 2-0 defeat to the Hammers, boos rang out around the King Power Stadium. During the match, supporters had chanted 'you don't know what you are doing,' after Puel made a double substitution, withdrawing Fousseni Diabate – who looked like one of the few Leicester players capable of posing a threat to the visitors from London that afternoon.

Only a thousand or so supporters stayed in their seats after the penultimate home game of the season, leading some pundits – including BBC *Match of the Day's* Martin Keown – to accuse the Foxes fan base of having 'short memories'. Tanner leapt to their defence. "City fans have been very loyal and very patient," he wrote. "It is unusual for them to turn in such an overwhelming fashion, and that is the real concern for Puel."

Puel sympathised with the supporters that had been critical of him in his post-match press conference. "In a difficult period, we always have some negativity and blame, it is normal," he said. "My focus is just to try to find good things and help my players to have a good reaction, and resolve this problem in this moment, and to resolve this situation."

He certainly achieved a good short-term solution, with Leicester claiming a 3-1 home win over Arsenal four days later, with Kelechi Iheanacho, Jamie Vardy and winger Riyad Mahrez – in what proved to be his final appearance at the King Power Stadium – on target. They ended the campaign with a defeat, going down 5-4 to Tottenham Hotspur at Wembley Stadium on May 13, 2018 in an entertaining but ultimately fruitless season finale for the Foxes.

The summer of 2018 proved to be a major period of change for Leicester City as Mahrez was sold to Manchester City for a club record £60m. Other members of the club's title-winning squad of 2015/16 departed, with Robert Huth announcing his retirement and Leonardo Ulloa signing for Mexican side Pachuca. The Foxes made a series of big-money purchases, with James Maddison and Ricardo Pereira both recruited for fees in excess of £20m. Other new arrivals included Jonny Evans, Danny Ward and Rachid Ghezzal.

Leicester's form in the early months of the 2018/19 season suggested they were on for another mid-table finish that campaign. Two wins in three in August against Wolverhampton Wanderers and Southampton saw the Foxes climb to seventh position, while they progressed to the League Cup third round with a 4-0 victory over Jamie Vardy's former club Fleetwood Town.

Back-to-back defeats to Liverpool and AFC Bournemouth followed in the Premier League before a 3-1 home triumph over Huddersfield Town on September 22, 2018. Three days later, Puel's team won a penalty shootout against Wolverhampton Wanderers to set up a fourth round meeting with his former employers Southampton in the League Cup. October began with two more league losses to Everton and Arsenal prior to the home fixture against West Ham United on October 27, 2018.

Vichai was present for the Hammers' visit to the King Power Stadium that evening. Tragically, it would be the last time the Foxes faithful would see their beloved chairman positioned in his customary seat in the front row of the Leicester City Directors Box.

Chapter Seven

Good Karma

The strength of Vichai Srivaddhanaprabha's Buddhist faith was obvious to anyone able to go behind the scenes at Leicester City on a matchday during his time as club owner and chairman. A group of monks from the Wat Traimit Withayaram Woraviharn (Golden Buddha) Temple in Bangkok's Chinatown were regularly flown to the East Midlands club to bless both the pitch and the players prior to kick-off, while the visiting congregation would spend the game meditating in a dedicated shrine room installed at the King Power Stadium.

"He's clearly very devout," Alex Hylton, Vichai's former personal assistant, told *The Telegraph* in a 2016 article. "It's obviously unusual for a football club owner to bring along Buddhist monks to games, but now everyone at LCFC is used to it. It seems normal.

"On important occasions he would fly in Buddhist monks for prayers before the game," expanded Hylton in another interview with *MailOnline* in 2016. "I remember at one time there were a dozen monks touring the ground, blessing the goal posts, the pitch and the changing rooms. There are marks of white paint all over the ground where the monks have blessed it.

"Vichai was the only person allowed to serve the monks. It was a real honour. They would then dine – you are not supposed to eat in front of a monk so they would eat separately - and either watch the game or meditate."

Vichai was a long-time devotee of the Wat Traimit temple's Phra Prommangkalachan, who became a monk at the age of 15. Shortly before the club's title success in 2016, Prommangkalachan was photographed with a pair of specially-made Leicester City pennants – featuring the Foxes crest together with Buddhist symbols – which were subsequently signed, blessed and given away.

MailOnline claims Vichai's Buddhist faith stemmed from his youth. He apparently borrowed £400 from his father as a youngster to buy four amulets for himself and his siblings. "After surviving a car accident, when he was wearing one around his neck, he became a serious collector and now owns £10m worth of Buddha sculptures, which are displayed in a museum at his Bangkok HQ," explained the article.

During Leicester City's season-of-seasons in 2015/16, Prommangkalachan – who some claim predicted the club's eventual Premier League title success months before it happened - spoke to *The Telegraph* about the support he and his temple offer the Foxes. "This is not about magic," he said. "We can only offer spiritual support. We believe that helps the players with their good health, with avoiding injuries, with their focus. But they must still perform well."

Asked about the ritual of meditating at the King Power Stadium during Leicester City matches, he added; "We know how Leicester are doing because the cheers and chanting rocks the room. We feel the vibrations."

Karma – action driven by intention which leads to future consequences – and 'Karamaphala' – the so-called 'fruit' of karmic acts – are fundamental concepts in Buddhism. Within the Wat Traimit Withayaram Woraviharn Temple and across Thailand as a whole, there is a popular belief that Vichai's "good deeds" helped generate good karma around Leicester City and secure the ultimate football Karamaphala – the Premier League title.

"Khun Vichai is a very strong and devoted Buddhist who has done many good works," Prommangkalachan told *The Telegraph*. "His good deeds help generate support which becomes power for Leicester City Football Club. The club is benefitting from that good karma. He is also a very wise man and knows how to manage the club, bring together the team and coaches and makes sure their approach is united. The result is their success."

Vichai used to fly the monks into London Southend Airport on a private plane, sometimes accompanying them on the same flight to or from Bangkok. Their support for the club was offered even when they weren't in the United Kingdom, with monks chanting and praying for the Foxes at their temple for all their fixtures, home and away.

Sky Sports News presenter Michelle Owen described Vichai as "a unique owner, renowned for his generosity to the fans with a clear understanding of how important they are to a football club." His kind deeds whilst Chairman of Leicester City often created news headlines – not only because of the acts themselves but because such philanthropy is relatively rare in the profit-driven industry of professional football.

While his generosity – the birthday gifts for supporters, the millions of pounds he would donate to good causes in the local area, etc – came as a surprise to many, a little research prior to Vichai's takeover of the club meant Foxes Trust chairman Ian Bason saw a man delivering on his promises... and then some!

"Prior to Vichai first arriving at Leicester City, I remember going on to the King Power website," recalled Bason. "There was a section on there that talked about the culture of the company and how they regularly gave money back into the community. It was quite a bold declaration and one that made an impact on me. Many organisations pay lip service to those kinds of things, but we would quickly discover with Vichai and King Power that they really did deliver."

Vichai's generosity in Leicester went way beyond free beer and cake on his birthday. At the club's annual awards night in 2016, it was announced via Foxes and King Power CEO, Susan Whelan, that the Thai businessman was to donate £2m to Leicester Hospitals Charity.

"It's very important for every fortunate thing that happens to you in your life, you must give back... That's really integral to everything we do," said Whelan. "This (donation) is through the Srivaddhanaprabha family, this is King Power, this is Leicester City Football Club saying thank you to the city of Leicester. You have opened your hearts to us. We are so very privileged and pleased to be a part of that."

"It was unbelievable," recalled Debbie Adlerstein, Head of Business Development at Leicester Hospitals Charity, on receiving news of the donation. "It was and is our largest donation to date. I can recall getting a phone call from Susan Whelan around 10pm that night. Susan told me 'I'm delighted to let you know that Vichai, personally, would like to donate £2m to the children's hospital adding 'I wanted to let you know as soon as possible because obviously the press will get hold of it'. That kind of generosity is almost unheard of and of course we were absolutely over the moon."

Vichai's gift has been allocated towards the construction costs of a Paediatric Intensive Care Unit (PICU), which will form part of a new £30m Children's Hospital at the Leicester Royal Infirmary.

"There has always been a good relationship between Leicester Hospitals Charity and Leicester City Football Club," added Adlerstein. "Since Vichai's takeover of the club though, the philanthropy from the club has increased massively. Vichai led from the top and showed he wasn't only prepared to put his hand in his pocket but to extend the fun of being involved with the football club to our patients. "He would donate a hospitality box at the King Power Stadium for matches, he organised parties and gifts for young patients. At the end of the season on a number of occasions, Vichai organised surplus stock from the club's shop to be sent to the charity rather than to sell it off more cheaply. He really did have the most incredible impact at the football club, across the city and of course here at the hospitals."

In the same week that Vichai announced he was to give away 60 free season tickets to Leicester City supporters in celebration of his 60th birthday, he threw a special teddy bear's picnic party for children at Leicester Hospital in April 2018. Susan Whelan was on hand to cut the cake, which carried the message 'Happy Birthday Mr Chairman', while first-team stars Kasper Schmeichel, Wilfred Ndidi and Kelechi Iheanacho were also in attendance.

"We invited long-term patients who come regularly to the hospital for a little treat," said Adlerstein. "They all had such a lovely time and were so excited. I think the most important thing is that they came to the hospital for a party, not to have treatments and not to have people look at them or anything scary – it was sheer fun."

Vichai regularly offered free match tickets to the hospitals charity as he did for staff and students at De Montfort University. He even donated £100,000 to the King Richard III Appeal in March 2015 to help fund the reburial of the monarch.

"The discovery of King Richard III's remains and the forthcoming reburial are events of enormous cultural and historical significance for Britain, made possible by the remarkable people of Leicester," said Vichai at the time. "It is a passionate community that frequently unites to support great causes - causes that bring great pride to the city and strengthen the bond between its people. As proud representatives of the city of Leicester, I am honoured to make this donation on behalf of Leicester City Football Club and our supporters."

Another of Vichai's major gifts to the local community came in the shape of a £1m donation to the University of Leicester's medical department. The LCFC Foxes Foundation – now known as the Vichai Srivaddhanaprabha Foundation - donated almost £2m to local charities under his chairmanship meanwhile.

"What struck me about those donations is that they were always made relatively quietly," commented Bason. "It was never done in a 'look what we've done' kind of way. These gestures were always understated and donations made with real class. You would often learn about work they'd done after it had happened rather than announcements being made beforehand."

Sports psychologist Ken Way, who worked with Leicester City during their title-winning season, echoes Bason's opinion that much of Vichai's philanthropic work went on without many people knowing about it.

"All the stories about what he did, charity-wise, giving away his money, I don't think they know 10% of what he did," Way once told the *Leicester Mercury*. "I did a talk on the outskirts of Leicester at an education establishment, I walked through the doors and there was a little plaque saying 'this building was built with donations by Vichai'. My wife is Thai and she tells me that everything that we experienced about him was true exactly as he did in Bangkok. The guy is a one-off."

When Leicester won promotion in 2014, he picked up the bill for a meal in a West End restaurant and gave each player and staff member a £1,000 chip to gamble at a nearby private members' club. After their Premier League triumph two years later, he forked out nearly £2m to buy 19 members of Claudio Ranieri's title-winning squad brand new BMW i8s.

Vichai's generosity extended beyond material gifts. Despite his hectic life schedule, there were many stories of how the Chairman was always there for his players and staff. Andy King, the Foxes longest-serving player under Vichai's reign described him as "a friend as much as a boss and a chairman." In a touching tribute to Vichai after his death, Kasper Schmeichel wrote; "You had time for everyone. You touched everyone. It didn't matter who it was, you had time for them. I always admired you as a leader, as a father and as a man."

Top summed up his father's person-centric approach to running a football club in an interview with *The Guardian*. "We give our time to the staff, the players and to the manager. We try to manage it like a family, to listen to the problems of every single member of staff," he said.

Sven-Goran Eriksson, who was Vichai's first managerial appointment, described the Thai to Sky Sports News as "a very good man" and echoed what Top has said about Leicester City under his father's chairmanship. "He treated the people at the club - players, staff, myself - in an extremely good way.

"I remember sometimes he invited me to London for meetings and, always in these meetings, he said 'now, we go out Sven, now we go to a good shop'. It was clothes for men and I said, 'I don't need anything,' but he said, 'yes, you need a jacket, you need this, you need that' - and he would never let me pay! He didn't need to do things like that, but that is how he was."

As well as treating his players and staff with the upmost care and attention, honouring and enhancing the history of Leicester City Football Club and donating to various institutions and charities, Vichai directly affected the lives of so many individuals …

Just before his fourth birthday in 2011, Leicester fan Ellis Page was diagnosed with MECP2 syndrome, a rare chromosome disorder that can cause both intellectual and muscular disability. Doctors told his parents that it was unlikely he would ever walk or talk — and would face daily seizures from epilepsy. His family started a fundraising campaign to help research a cure for the condition, with sponsored bike rides to Leicester away matches across the country. Vichai heard of their efforts. In 2014, Sky News reported he had donated £22,000. It subsequently transpired that the donation was actually £44,000, pushing their fundraising efforts over the £100,000 mark. Further funds were raised when Leicester City donated players' shirts from their Championship title-winning season of 2013/14 to be auctioned.

On February 25, 2018, the city of Leicester was rocked by the news of an explosion at a shop on Hinckley Road. It transpired that five people in the property - Mary Ragoobar, her sons Shane and Sean and Leah Beth Reek, Shane's girlfriend as well as 22-year-old shop worker Viktorija Ijevleva died in the blast. Jose Ragoobeer – who lost his wife and two sons in the explosion – told *Pukaar News* how Vichai supported him in the aftermath of the tragedy.

"I was looking for a venue for the wake and a relative told me that they would speak to the (Leicester City) Chairman and see if they could support me in any way," he said. "They (the Srivaddhanaprabhas) provided the hall with all of the facilities, food and everything and it was a great help, a massive help for me. All of the staff and the ambassador Alan Birchenall were very kind and supportive and from that you can see how the owners make it (Leicester City) like a family."

One of Vichai's many friends in the travel retail industry was Martin Moodie, the Founder and Chairman of the *Moodie Davitt Report*. The King Power International Company hosted The Trinity Forum – the world's leading airport commercial revenues event – alongside the *Moodie Davitt Report* at Vichai's Pullman Bangkok King Power Hotel in 2011. On the first day of the event, Moodie – who was in the early weeks of recovery from stomach cancer and related surgery – was taken seriously ill with post-operative, life-endangering complications.

"Khun Vichai personally oversaw that I was treated at the world-class Bumrumgrad International Hospital, but, even more, that his personal physician led my care and visited me each day," recalled Moodie in the *Moodie Davitt Report*. "After my release a week later, he insisted that I - and a New Zealand friend who flew over to act as my carer - stay at the Pullman Bangkok King Power Hotel as his guests until I was fit enough to fly home. I was not treated as an industry executive but as a family friend."

BBC Radio Leicester commentator and reporter Ian Stringer only ever interviewed Vichai twice during his chairmanship of Leicester City, yet every matchday at the King Power Stadium, the owner always went over to say 'hello' to him and shake his hand. A few years after taking over the club, the Srivaddhanaprabha family surprised Stringer with a kind gesture during a visit to Thailand.

"I was back in Bangkok in 2012, running the city's marathon to raise money for charity," Stringer told BBC Sport. "Top not only donated £1,000, he also offered a room in the King Power hotel and sent a car to take me to the start line at 3am and back afterwards. He also arranged for a meal for me afterwards."

Alan Birchenall told the *Leicester Mercury* of Vichai's kindness after he suffered a cardiac arrest in 2017. "I remember waking up in my room in Glenfield Hospital, and rather than just a bowl of fruit and a few flowers there was half a rainforest and a whole fruit stall (sent by Vichai)," he said. "When I returned to work, he used to pop in to see me in my office at the training ground and ask: 'Are you still here Birch?', 'Still here Mr Chairman!' 'I can't get rid of you'. He had a wicked sense of humour."

Birchenall was presented with a lifetime contract during Vichai's time at the club, in recognition of his loyalty to Leicester City. That kind of gesture was typical of a chairman who respected not only deserving individuals but the heritage and the history of Leicester City Football Club.

"Fans repeatedly spoke of Khun Vichai as 'one of us' – a real football fan," wrote Steve Moulds in the Foxes Trust newsletter. "He understood that fans mattered to his club and that the club mattered to Leicester as a community."

A proud Leicester City supporter, Vichai was always keen to promote both Thailand and Thai values too. He contributed as generously in his homeland as he did in his adopted city of Leicester. In 2017, he launched a countrywide campaign in Thailand called 'Sport Power', which pledged to donate one million footballs to children and build 100 artificial football pitches. This followed on from his creation of 'Fox Hunt' – a scholarship programme, which enabled a select group of Thai footballers, under the age of the 15, to join Leicester City's academy for a 30-month period and study at a local boarding school. A total of 16 players were part of the club's first intake in 2014, with further groups joining the programme in 2017 and 2018. According to *The Nation*, each player attending the scholarship programme came at an estimated cost of Bt15m (£350,000) to King Power.

Shortly after Leicester won the Premier League title in 2016, he told reporters in Bangkok of his other major footballing dream. "I'd like to see Thailand secure their first ever World Cup berth in 10 years," he said, explaining his ambition as one of the reasons for creating 'Fox Hunt'. Sadly, he will never see the fruits of that particular karmic act.

Chapter Eight

Into the Light

The first line of Peter Schmeichel's letter to Vichai Srivaddhanaprabha – written hours after Leicestershire Police confirmed the death of the Leicester City Chairman – summed up the thoughts and feelings of many. "Dear Mr Chairman, I cannot believe this is happening," it said.

Schmeichel said he was "totally devastated and heartbroken" – sentiments that certainly rang true for the people of Leicester, who had witnessed a civic and footballing fairy tale end in an unthinkable nightmare.

In the hours and days after the disaster, there was outpouring of emotion from the local community who headed, en masse, to lay tributes to Vichai and the other crash victims. His impact beyond the Leicestershire area was evident too, with shirts and scarves laid at the King Power Stadium by supporters of other football clubs – including rivals Derby County and Nottingham Forest. A message on a shirt left by a Wolverhampton Wanderers supporter read 'divided by colours, united by grief'. The 'football family' had truly been rocked by the tragedy.

Leicester City players and staff joined supporters at the King Power Stadium on October 29, 2018, as did Vichai's son Top and widow Aimon. The pair laid a wreath in memory of Vichai in the centre circle of the pitch before observing the ever-growing mass of tributes outside the ground. The stadium scoreboards illuminated images of the club's beloved former Chairman with the simple words, 'Rest in Peace'. A book of condolence was opened at the King Power Stadium as well as online that same day.

Three days after the crash, a vigil was held by supporters at the King Power Stadium at 8:37pm – the exact time of the incident on October 27, 2018. A two minute silence was followed by two minutes applause. There were tributes elsewhere too. De Montfort University staged both a minute of silence and a minute's applause on their campus in Hawthorn Square. Vice-Chancellor Professor Dominic Shellard heralded Vichai's impact at both the football club and the wider community of Leicester and added; "We cherish our university's long-standing partnership with Leicester City, which has delivered so much for us through our joint efforts, often at the prompting of the owner."

The University of Leicester held a similar tribute outside their Fielding Johnson Building while Vichai's image and the words 'Thank You Vichai' adorned the cover of the winter 2018 edition of Leicester Hospital's *Together* magazine. "Vichai was indeed an extremely special individual, not only with his involvement with the football club, but the effort he made to engage with fans and the community of Leicester," wrote the hospital's Chief Executive John Adler.

In addition to Leicester City's postponement of their League Cup and Under-23s' Premier League International Cup fixtures in the week that followed the tragedy, Foxes' sister club OH Leuven announced that their league match with Lommel at the Den Dreef Stadium had been rescheduled. The wider football community paid its respects in the meantime, with a minute of silence held before Premier League games at Burnley, Crystal Palace and Manchester United on October 28, 2018 both in tribute to Vichai and ahead of Remembrance Day.

The following evening, ex-Leicester City player Riyad Mahrez gave Manchester City a 1-0 victory over Tottenham Hotspur at Wembley Stadium and subsequently dedicated his goal to Vichai.

"The boss (Vichai) was very special to me," Mahrez told Sky Sports after the match. "I spent four and a half years there (at Leicester City) and have many memories with him. He was such a good person and had a big heart. It was heart-breaking and shocking for me to hear this news and for all of the other people who died with him. I am with Leicester and the family of the victims."

On November 2, Vichai's body was returned home to Thailand for a royal-sponsored funeral ceremony. The bodies of Kaveporn Punpare and Nusara Suknamai were also flown to their homeland while the funerals of pilots Eric Swaffer and his partner Izabela Lechowicz took place on November 22. The couple also had a service held in their memory at Guildford Cathedral on December 6. The service had to be moved from their local church in Camberley to the cathedral to accommodate around 1,000 people that came from all over the globe to pay their respects.

Members of Vichai's family accompanied his coffin home from Leicester on a private jet which arrived at Don Mueang Airport. Waiting vehicles immediately took them to Sala Kawi Niramit Debsirindrawas Temple in the Pom Prap Sattru Phai District of Bangkok. The funeral service began with a bathing ritual, using royally-bestowed water.

Back in the United Kingdom, Leicester's first match after the tragedy was always going to be an emotional occasion.

The Foxes' visit to Cardiff City on November 3 was succinctly described by BBC Sport Wales' Dafydd Pritchard as "an afternoon when football seemed both an irrelevance and a form of release for Leicester's grieving players and fans".

Amidst a sombre and respectful atmosphere, a joint flag with the club crests of Cardiff City and Leicester City and the words 'R.I.P Vichai' as well as the Thailand national flag, was passed around the Cardiff City Stadium by both home and away supporters. Wreaths were laid too, while a minute of silence – which also honoured the other four victims of the disaster – was impeccably observed.

Despite the rawness of emotion flooding the Welsh capital, the match itself was as keenly contested as any other Premier League fixture. The Bluebirds struck the crossbar from a Victor Camarasa free-kick while the visitors felt unfortunate not to be awarded with a penalty, when a Jamie Vardy shot appeared to hit Cardiff defender Sol Bamba's arm in the 18-yard-box.

The breakthrough came ten minutes into the second period when Demari Gray hit a low shot past Neil Etheridge to give Leicester the lead. The entire team celebrated together before running to the away supporters. Gray removed his shirt to reveal another t-shirt that was emblazoned with the words 'For Khun Vichai'. The final whistle heralded victory for the Foxes and another touching moment between players, staff and fans, who applauded each other after the game, with Vichai clearly in the forefront of their thoughts.

In his post-match interview, goalkeeper Kasper Schmeichel commented; "That was a tough game not just on the pitch but mentally. There are a lot of exhausted people in there now but I am proud of this team and the club, the way everyone has handled themselves has been unbelievable. We were very lucky to know Khun Vichai.

"Today was difficult, coming out for the warm-up was tough, the first 10 minutes I couldn't steady myself, I was shaking a little bit. But it was nice to get a win to take to Thailand now and hopefully we did his family proud."

After their victory in Cardiff, the players headed to Bangkok to attend part of Vichai's week-long funeral. Upon their evening arrival at the temple, the players offered their condolences to his wife Aimon and children Voramas, Apichet, Aroonroong and Aiyawatt. The squad then joined the Srivaddhanaprabha family for the Abhidhamma Recitations Ceremony, the chanting of the Higher Teachings of the Buddha.

The temple was adorned with a floral tribute to Vichai while an eight-sided urn was bestowed upon the ceremony by Thailand's King Maha Vajiralongkorn. The Srivaddhanaprabha family requested no funeral wreaths to be sent but instead invited donations to be made to the Navamindrapobitr 84th Anniversary Building at the Siriraj Hospital. The Leicester City players spent around 36 hours in Bangkok prior to returning to the United Kingdom to prepare for their first home match since their Chairman's passing, against Burnley on November 10. Vichai's funeral finished the day before that fixture.

At 12:45pm on the day of the game against the Clarets, thousands took to the streets of Leicester to take part in the so-called '5,000-1 Walk' to honour the five people who died in the helicopter crash the previous month. The brainchild of young Foxes supporters Megan Elliott, 14, and her sister

Casey, 11, the walk's name played on Leicester's title-odds ahead of the 2015/16 season. The sisters originally appealed for 5,000 people to take part in the event, which followed a route from Jubilee Square via De Montfort University and on to the King Power Stadium. It was obvious from a quick glance that a far greater number, including Foxes players and staff, were in attendance. Indeed, Leicestershire Police and Leicester City Council, who helped manage the huge event, estimated that some 50,000 people participated.

Megan Elliott spoke of her delight at the turnout to the BBC. "I never thought it would end up this big," she said. "When we met Vichai in Madrid (ahead of the Foxes' UEFA Champions League match against Atletico Madrid) he was lovely, cheerful and happy. Today shows how loved and respected he was. Not just by the club but by the entire community."

Supporters were advised by Leicester City to take their seats by 2:35pm prior to the sell-out match against Burnley. A special tribute video to Vichai was played on the big screens at the King Power Stadium, which brought many fans to tears. The club's former managers Claudio Ranieri and Nigel Pearson as well as Martin O'Neill watched on from the stands.

In a type of gesture made so typically by Vichai during his lifetime, Leicester City provided visitors to the King Power Stadium on that poignant day with commemorative pin badges, clap banners and programmes. Scarves were also issued to supporters free of charge, displaying the words 'FOREVER IN OUR HEARTS' on one side and 'MR CHAIRMAN' on the other. Players warmed up in t-shirts that carried an image of Vichai and his popular nickname at the club, 'The Boss'.

A two minute silence was held prior to kick-off in memory of the crash victims as well as to mark the upcoming Remembrance Day. The players wore shirts with Vichai's name emblazoned on them for the first-half, changing into shirts with an embroidered poppy symbol for the second period.

The match itself saw Leicester make a bright start, with a Jamie Vardy shot cleared off the line by a Burnley defender while Rachid Ghezzal struck the Clarets' goalframe. Former England international Joe Hart made a save at the feet of Demarai Gray as the Leicester onslaught continued in the first period. Perhaps unsurprisingly, given the mental and physical exertions of the past two weeks - which included the 12,000-mile round trip to Bangkok for Vichai's funeral - the Foxes' pressure diminished in the second half. A goalless draw was a fair result on a day when football still seemed of secondary importance.

A statement from Leicester City and the Srivaddhanaprabha family prior to the visit of Burnley to the King Power Stadium summed up their thoughts and emotions.

"The Srivaddhanaprabha family and everyone at Leicester City Football Club have been deeply moved by the remarkable volume of generous and thoughtful tributes left at King Power Stadium," it read. "The extraordinary scenes of compassion and condolence demonstrated on Filbert Way in the last week have been an enormous source of comfort and strength to the families involved and to everyone whose lives have been touched by recent events. The support of our fans, our community and the football world during this darkest of weeks will never be forgotten."

Days before the match against Burnley, the European Aviation Safety Agency (EASA) released an 'Airworthiness Directive', which demanded checks of all tails of all AgustaWestland AW169 and AW189 helicopters as a precautionary measure. The EASA subsequently issued an 'Emergency Alert Service Bulletin', requiring the periodic inspection of the tail rotor system.

Air Accidents Investigation Branch's (AAIB) Bulletin S1/2018 was published on November 14 outlining the progress of the investigation into the tragedy; "Investigation of the tail rotor control system is being carried out as a priority," said the AAIB in a three-page report. In its second bulletin, released on December 6, the AAIB revealed the helicopter lost control because the tail rotor actuator control shaft became disconnected from the actuator lever mechanism.

On November 28, the Duke and Duchess of Cambridge visited the King Power Stadium to pay tribute to Vichai – a man Prince William knew personally from the polo scene in England. "We knew Vichai as a man who cared deeply about his family and also his community," commented the Duke. "He of course was a man of wealth, but that wealth did not leave him disconnected from those around him." The couple met Vichai's wife, Aimon, as well his daughter Aroonroong and son, Top with William revealing that that he had previously "had the privilege" to fly with the deceased pilot Eric Swaffer.

As the 2018/19 football season continued, Vichai was never far from the thoughts of Leicester City fans and indeed away supporters attending matches at the King Power. Members of the 1881 Movement, a Watford fan group, raised over £2,500 to produce a banner – displayed prior to the Foxes home match with the Hornets on December 1 which read; 'Thank you Vichai for allowing us all to dream. Rest in Peace'.

Manchester City supporters followed suit, raising a banner which read 'Brothers in Blue, RIP Vichai' during a League Cup quarter final tie at the King Power Stadium on December 18. Alas, the Foxes lost 3-1 on penalties that evening, as they were eliminated from the Carabao Cup. Leicester paid a fitting tribute to Vichai on the pitch around the Christmas period, securing the club's first win at Chelsea in 18 years with a 1-0 triumph at Stamford Bridge on December 22. This was followed by a 2-1 triumph over Manchester City on Boxing Day.

The results were high points in a season of emotional struggle for everyone connected with Leicester City. Many players, including those at youth team level, attended one-on-one counselling sessions provided by the club. The Professional Footballers' Association and the Sporting Chance Clinic also reached out to the Foxes to offer emotional support.

Then-Leicester manager Claude Puel said he had been left "numb and in shock" after the tragedy. "This has been without doubt one of the hardest weeks in the history of this football club," said Puel. "The tragic loss of five lives has left us numb and in shock and our prayers and love remain with Vichai's family and with the all of the families who have lost a loved one. Vichai made Leicester City into what it is. He made it a family and made a dream. He invested in the club, the city and he invested in the people."

In his column for *The Mirror* newspaper, former Leicester City player Robbie Savage wrote that the collapse of Glenn Hoddle on his *Saturday Morning Savage* show and the death of Vichai made him "re-evaluate my whole life". He revealed he had been referred to a counsellor after the shock events and added "I have no time for negativity any more. Life is too precious. But this is not about me."

In his tribute to the late Leicester City Chairman, Savage wrote; "When people talk about Leicester's 5,000-1 long-shots pulling off the greatest miracle in the history of football, it was Vichai who gave the people a reason to dream anything was possible. He didn't just give everyone connected with a football club belief that they could achieve the impossible – he transformed a whole city's outlook."

The crash of October 27 came just days after the 22nd anniversary of a helicopter crash which claimed the life of Matthew Harding – then Vice-Chairman of Chelsea Football Club – along with Ray Deane, Tony Burridge, John Bauldie and Mick Goss. They had been travelling back from the Blues' League Cup tie at Bolton Wanderers when their aircraft came down at Middlewich in Cheshire on October 22, 1996.

Tragically, the football community was to be affected by another aviation disaster during the 2018/19 season, when a Piper PA-46 Malibu plane carrying Argentinian striker Emiliano Sala crashed off Alderney in the English Channel on January 21, 2019. The flight was bound for Cardiff from Nantes, with Sala having recently signed for Cardiff City Football Club. The body of the 28-year-old was recovered on February 7, 2019. At the time of writing, pilot David Ibbotson remained missing and presumed dead.

Cardiff City had shown impeccable class in helping Leicester City pay tribute to Vichai in their first match after his death.

The Foxes pledged their own support to the Welsh club after the disappearance and subsequent passing of Sala.

"It's important to be close with them (Cardiff City) and to support them in this powerful tragedy at the club," said Puel. "It's difficult all the time to have to manage this situation. We know this situation in the past. I have thoughts for the families of the player (Sala), for the fans, and for the club in France they have had time to know him, he was a nice person and of course, it's a difficult thing to think. We give all our support for the club and we know they can have spirit in this moment."

Sala's funeral was held in his home town of San Martin de Progreso in Argentina on February 16, 2019 with Bluebirds manager Neil Warnock amongst those present.

Vichai's funeral finished on November 9, 2018, after which his body was kept in the Sala Kawi Niramit Debsirindrawas Temple for 100 days – as is Buddhist tradition - until a cremation ceremony on March 21, 2019. Leicester City players and staff flew to Thailand to pay their final respects to 'The Boss' for that ceremony, with the King of Thailand, His Majesty Maha Vajiralongkorn Bodindradebayavarangkun also present.

Chapter Nine

Vichai's Legacy

As Leicester City supporters arrived at the King Power Stadium for the first home match after Khun Vichai's passing, they will have noticed a rainbow illuminating the grey skies above them. Such symbolism further enhanced the belief amongst the Foxes faithful that the man they call 'The Boss' will forever watch over them.

In practical terms, Vichai's legacy at Leicester City looks certain to live on, with future plans he had for the club remaining very much in the pipeline. In a matchday programme article a few months before his death, he vowed to make the Foxes a "sustainable and consistently competitive force in the Premier League". His vision for the club included the expansion of the King Power Stadium and the construction of a new, £100m training complex – with planning permission approved for the latter project.

Vichai's son Top has always stressed that Leicester City is a long-term project for the Srivaddhanaprabha family. At a press conference shortly after the Asia Football Investments consortium had purchased the club, the then-25-year-old fielded a question from BBC Radio Leicester's Ian Stringer as to where he hoped to be in five years. "Celebrating my 30th birthday at the (King Power) Stadium," he responded. Even in the most unthinkable of circumstances, Top has vowed that King Power and the Srivaddhanaprabhas' influence at the club will continue.

"My dad had a way of teaching me about life and work without making it seem like a lesson. He was my mentor and role model," he wrote, in a statement published on October 31, 2018. "Today, he has left me with a legacy to continue and I will do everything I can to carry on his big vision and dreams."

"Our continued growth as a club, our state-of-the-art new training ground and our planned stadium expansion will help realise his vision for Leicester City," added Top in a matchday programme article.

Leicester's proposed 185-acre training complex, situated off the A46 some eight miles north of the city, has been designed by KSS and will incorporate 12 full-size football pitches, including a covered show pitch with 499 seats and an elevated camera platform. There will also be hydrotherapy, medical, rehabilitation and dining facilities on site as well as 30 bedrooms for players and staff.

"The new training ground is a truly exciting phase of our development and a once-in-a-generation opportunity to demonstrate our ambition," commented Top in a 2018 statement. "We want to invest in the best possible training facilities to develop and attract the world's elite sporting talent to Leicester and to give them a competitive edge in a game that is constantly evolving.

"It is crucial to us that the benefits brought about by the new development make the facility a source of pride for the Leicestershire community - known for so many years for its rich tradition in sporting development."

With regards to the expansion of the King Power Stadium, the project specifics and timescale are a little less clear. Top mentioned the possibility of increasing the capacity to around 42,000 back in 2015 but he and the club have been less clear in recent times with regards to the number of seats they would like to add. Of the four stands at the ground, the redevelopment is most likely to involve the East Stand first.

"It (stadium expansion) is something we have thought about a lot over the last eight years, but we had to be sure that the club was ready to take that step and that it was consistent with the sustainable growth of the club," wrote Vichai in a matchday programme article during the 2018/19 season.

"The King Power Stadium atmosphere has been such a big asset to Leicester City during that time that we had to make sure any possible expansion would be good for the matchday experience and the advantage it gives to the team on the pitch."

"The plan is to increase capacity and upgrade facilities for the stadium itself, and invest in the surrounding site to create an exciting events destination for the city of Leicester," added Top.

A club museum has been discussed as part of the club's stadium expansion plans, which could serve as a home to the non-floral tributes, such as football shirts and scarves, left outside the King Power Stadium following Vichai's death. "It is the club's intention to incorporate such artefacts into the planned redevelopment and expansion of King Power Stadium - a project Khun Vichai announced on his 60th birthday," confirmed a club statement.

Another likely future addition at the King Power Stadium is a statue of Vichai, which Top announced his plans to commission to serve as a "permanent and fitting tribute to the man that made it all possible".

Vichai once said that; "A football club means nothing without its fans and we will continue to keep you at the heart of every decision we make for your club," and that "we must never allow the family essence of our club to be lost." The Srivaddhanaprabhas have been true to those words throughout their time at Leicester City, forging a harmonious relationship with Foxes supporters that seems relatively unique compared to fans and owners at other professional football clubs.

Ian Bason, chairman of the Foxes Trust, says the Thai family are "100% admired and trusted" by Leicester City supporters, citing an open discourse between the board and the Trust as well as a "high level of respect" between club and supporters.

"A good example of that is a consultation the club organised over the summer of 2018 with regards to the future expansion of Leicester City," added Bason. "That was run through a consultancy company, meaning nobody from Leicester City was present and thus, had no influence over what was discussed. That was certainly managed very well."

Away from Leicester City Football Club, Vichai's legacy lives on in various forms. Cowdray Park Polo Club announced the launch of the Vichai Srivaddhanaprabha Memorial Cup towards the end of 2018. The trophy is presented to the winning team of the quarter final match in the King Power Gold Cup for the British Open Polo Championship on an annual basis.

Another tribute to Vichai exists in the shape of a stunning oil on canvas portrait of the late King Power owner by Leicester artist Paul Wright called 'Father'. It was unveiled at a Thai photo exhibition at the New Walk Museum in 2019, next to which the Leicester museum service displayed its own tribute to the billionaire which read; "Leicester Arts, Museums and Festivals Service wishes to respectfully dedicate this exhibition to the memory of founder and CEO of the King Power company and Chairman of Leicester City Football Club Vichai Srivaddhanaprabha 1958–2018."

In the months following Vichai's death, the Srivaddhanaprabha family and Top in particular had the tough task of continuing his business legacy and ensuring the smooth running of King Power. In November 2018, Reuters reported on the organisation's defeat in its bid for a retail and services concession for the new U-Tapao International Airport in Thailand's eastern province of Rayong. The contract was instead awarded to Central Department Store Company (Central Group) and DFS Group (through DFS Venture Singapore).

King Power did manage to secure a ten-year duty-free agreement at the airport, but the split concession model – dividing duty-free and retail operations - represented a major switch in the bidding process the organisation had been used to. U-Tapao is the first airport in Thailand to hold an auction with multiple concessions, splitting up duty free and retail operations," explained Reuters. "Up until now, King Power has enjoyed near monopoly, being a sole operator with concessions in all major airports."

King Power's most lucrative franchise at the time of writing is at Suvarnabhumi Airport. That single-licence contract is set to expire in 2020, with the next bidding tender due to follow the split concession model. Outlining the future challenges facing Top and King Power, Nattabhorn Juengsanguansit, Director at Asia Group Advisors - a government affairs consultancy, told Reuters;

"(King Power) has a successful history in duty free retailing and the travel industry, now the question is how effective King Power can be in engaging the government and other stakeholders without Vichai's leadership, especially in upcoming auctions for concessions in Bangkok, Phuket, Pattaya and Samut Prakan. Winning the upcoming bid is crucial for King Power's business and the future of Leicester football club."

A politician with "close ties with the Srivaddhanaprabha family," commented in the same article "Top has been his father's apprentice for more than ten years so he must have learnt a lot of his trade".

Vichai's son has certainly not shied away from making big decisions since his father's death, especially those relating to Leicester City Football Club. On February 24, 2019, the Foxes announced the sacking of manager Claude Puel after 16 months in charge at the King Power Stadium. Writing in the club programme for their home fixture against Brighton & Hove Albion two days later, Top commented;

"Following Saturday's defeat here against Crystal Palace (February 23, 2019) - not simply the result itself, but the circumstances and feeling surrounding it - it was clear to me that, regrettably, a change of manager would be necessary to keep the Club moving in the right direction.

"It's never an easy thing to do. It's always been my preference to give a manager time to overcome challenges and develop a squad that can grow stronger together and make progress through shared improvement and experience."

There were certainly mixed views amongst Leicester City fans regarding Puel's team selections, style of football and the overall progress that was made during the Frenchman's time at the club. What was not in doubt were his personal qualities, which were highlighted following Vichai's death and which were touched upon by Top in his article.

"I'm personally grateful to Claude Puel for all his work in the last 16 months," wrote Top. "His faith and willingness to give opportunities to young talent during a time of transition for the Club has helped us to develop an exciting young group of players that I'm sure will have a big role in the Club's future. He has also been a good man and a strong leader during some difficult times, showing dignity, compassion and an understanding of the family ethos we have at Leicester City, which will not be forgotten by anyone here."

Puel - who took charge of 67 Leicester City games in all competitions and led the Foxes to 23 wins - released a statement through the League Managers' Association on his departure from the King Power Stadium, which read; "It was my honour to work for the late and much loved Khun Vichai, who gave me the fantastic opportunity to manage his club and share some great moments with him.

"My mission at Leicester City Football Club ends here but I will continue to follow the performances of the team and wish the club all the best for the future."

On February 26, 2019, Leicester City announced Brendan Rodgers as Puel's replacement. The former Watford, Reading, Swansea City and Liverpool manager left Celtic – where he had won the domestic 'Treble' two seasons running – to take the Foxes role.

"I'd just like to say that I'm very privileged and honoured to be here as the manager," the Northern Irishman told LCFC TV on his appointment. "I promise that I'll give my life to making them proud of their team and proud of their club, and I look forward to working with them because together we're stronger.

"It's been a really difficult period, like I say, but my message is that together we'll be stronger and on and off the pitch let's make the right steps forward and I look forward to, like I say, making them proud of their team."

Rodgers' team were beaten 2-1 at his former club Watford in his first match as Foxes manager on March 3 but bounced back six days later with a 3-1 home victory over Fulham. A 2-1 win at Burnley on March 16 came shortly before the manager, staff and players departed for Thailand to attend Vichai's cremation service.

"Watching from the outside in and then coming into the club, to get a real sense of what he, Vichai, meant to everyone, he was an incredible leader," commented Rodgers before the squad's trip to Bangkok. "For all his wealth he was a good person. I always say the best people you meet, and the best coaches are normally the best people. I don't know him but speaking to Top, it is my job to try to create the values of the Chairman and use that as a building block for the club going forward, and the many great values he did have."

Rodgers, who described Top as "brave and so courageous" at "a really dark time for him", suffered his own heartbreak, losing both his parents at a relatively young age. His mum Christina died suddenly in 2010 at the age of 53 while his father lost his long battle against throat cancer just 18 months later. "People will understand what that experience does to you and how tough it was, especially if you were close to your father," commented Rodgers on Top's loss.

"You can be young but have lots of experience, so he'll (Top) be on a learning curve as well," added Rodgers. "It's an exponential curve he's on, and he's been doing a lot in his father's shadow for many years so he'll understand it. But, of course, when the curtain goes back and the light is shining on you, it's different."

During the 2018/19 season, Leicester City supporters sang the club's anthem *When You're Smiling* at the 60-minute mark of matches in honour of Vichai, who was 60 when he died. They also chanted their own version of the Bahamian folk song *Sloop John B* - which was adapted and recorded by The Beach Boys in 1966 – with the lyrics;

"Vichai had a dream,
"To build our football team,
"He came from Thailand and now he's one of our own,
"We play from the back, we counter attack,
"Champions of England, you made us sing that."

Vichai's name will live on forever more at Leicester City Football Club and in the local community. "I think his legacy will be bringing the city (of Leicester) so much joy," Radio Gwendolen's Renuka Odedra told online broadcaster *Copa90* shortly after his passing. Of the Foxes miracle Premier League title success, local Sky Sports reporter Rob Dorsett said; "It was Vichai who put all the right people in the right roles. It was Vichai who motivated them, who believed it was all possible, who told them to dream big. It was Vichai who made footballing fantasy, a reality. And that will be his legacy."

And Ken Way, the psychologist that worked so closely with the Leicester City title-winning side of 2015/16 heralded Vichai as "such a sweet, gentle guy".

"He was always there but never pushing," said Way in an interview with *MailOnline*. "One word I used to describe him

141

to people who didn't know him, and I mean this positively, was 'unassuming'. I mean it really positively. You have a guy who is a billionaire and he could throw his weight around but he never, ever did that."

To the Foxes Trust and Leicester City supporters, Vichai is "one of their own". "He will be fondly remembered for his achievements on the pitch but, moreover, it was his humbleness and dignity that really endeared him to the people of Leicester," commented Bason.

"While fan-owned clubs are the ideal scenario for most football supporters, I think that is an impossibility at Premier League level. King Power have proven to be dream owners. For me, the key legacy that Vichai leaves is the inspiration and the blueprint for other owners at other clubs. He has set the benchmark for the right and proper way to run a football club.

"Obviously, there were associated benefits for Vichai running a football club... it enhances King Power's global reputation for one thing. But he wasn't running a football club to make money. Vichai did what he did for the love of football. Many owners simply see the football club as an investment but Vichai wasn't like that.

"What he did was multi-faceted. He improved the fortunes of the club but he also delivered for the local community. He got involved in local charities. Many owners have made certain gestures to their supporters but generally, there's a lack of relationship with fans and they alienate them in some cases. At Leicester City, there is a clear synergy between supporters and the club and Vichai was hugely responsible for creating that."

On April 4, 2019 – which would have marked Vichai's 61st birthday – another major legacy in the late Leicester City Chairman's name was created. The newly-named Vichai Srivaddhanaprabha Foundation allocated £610,000 to charities and good causes as part of a campaign called 'Gift of a Wish'. Priority was given to those in the East Midlands/Leicestershire area.

"Khun Vichai's benevolence and generous acts were as varied as they were plentiful and it's important that his Foundation continues in that spirit," said Leicester City CEO Susan Whelan in a statement. "He treated modest causes with the same respect and dignity that he showed to major beneficiaries and it is in that manner that we will continue to support those in need in our community.

"He cared deeply about people and their impact within the community."

As Vichai cared so greatly for other people, so they cared for him. Leicester City's Premier League title success in 2015/16, along with his philanthropy in Leicestershire, Thailand and elsewhere, was proof of his ability to make dreams come true. After the nightmare of October 27, 2018, thousands flocked to the King Power Stadium to remember an individual who managed to captivate hearts and minds despite him keeping a low public profile for so much of his life.

While there remains a sense of collective loss across the city of Leicester especially, the greatest heartbreak belongs to the Srivaddhanaprabha family. "I miss you dad, with all of my heart," wrote Vichai's son and heir apparent Top at the end of an emotional tribute to his father.

Author's Note

Andy Greeves is a freelance football journalist and a regular contributor to matchday programmes across the Premier League, EFL Championship and national associations. Andy's work has also appeared in *The Guardian*, *The Observer* and *FourFourTwo* magazine while he is the author of the official Birmingham City and Tottenham Hotspur annuals. His debut biography, *Harry Kane: Golden Boy* was published in 2018.

Follow @AndyGreeves on Twitter.